Kyrgyzstan

Postcommunist States and Nations

Books in the series

Belarus: a denationalized nation
David R. Marples

Armenia: at the crossroads
Joseph R. Masih and Robert O. Krikorian

Poland: the conquest of history
George Sanford

Kyrgyzstan: central asia's island of democracy?
John Anderson

Kyrgyzstan

CENTRAL ASIA'S ISLAND OF DEMOCRACY?

John Anderson

Routledge
Taylor & Francis Group

LONDON AND NEW YORK

2 Park Square, Milton Park, Abingdon, Oxon, OX14 4RN
270 Madison Ave, New York NY 10016

Transferred to Digital Printing 2007

British Library Cataloguing in Publication Data

Anderson, John
 Kyrgyzstan: central Asia's island of democracy? – (Postcommunist states & nations; v. 4)
 1. Kyrgyzstan – History 2. Kyrgyzstan – Politics and government
 3. Kyrgyzstan – Economic conditions
 I. Title
 958.4'3

 ISBN 90-5702-390-3 (softcover)

Publisher's Note
The publisher has gone to great lengths to ensure the quality of this reprint but points out that some imperfections in the original may be apparent

FOR MY PARENTS, PETER AND AUDREY ANDERSON,
WHO CONSTANTLY SUPPORTED ME IN MY ECCENTRIC INTELLECTUAL
PURSUITS, AND IN MEMORY OF JANE ELLIS,
WHO TAUGHT ME MUCH AND, FAR MORE IMPORTANTLY,
PROVIDED A VOICE FOR SO MANY.

TABLE OF CONTENTS

Chronology ix

Preface xi

Map of Kyrgyzstan xvii

1 From Nomads to Citizens: The Genesis of Independent
Statehood 1

2 Island of Democracy? The Politics of Independence 23

3 The Switzerland of the East: Economic Reform in Kyrgyzstan 65

4 Kyrgyz Security in a Post-Soviet Era 85

Bibliography 103

Index 105

CHRONOLOGY

1775	First Kyrgyz embassy to Russia
c. 1830	Last Kyrgyz tribes accept suzereignty of Kokand
1862	Kyrgyz soldiers help Russians to take Pishpek
1864	Birth of Toktogul Saltylganov
1876	Kyrgyz territory subordinate to Russia
1898	Andizhan revolt
1916	Steppe revolt
March 1917	First soviet appears in Kyzyl-Kiia
December 1917	Soviet power established in Talas
1924	Creation of Kara-Kyrgyz Autonomous Oblast within RSFSR
1927	Creation of Kyrgyz Autonomous Soviet Socialist Republic
1927	Khudzhum launched to liberate the women of Central Asia
1936	Creation of Kyrgyz Soviet Socialist Republic
1938	Trial and execution of leading Kyrgyz politicians and cultural figures
1961	Appointment of Turdakun Usubaliev as Kyrgyz first secretary
1985	Absamat Masaliev appointed first secretary
1989	Formation of Ashar
September 1989	Adoption of state language law
2 February 1990	Elections to Supreme Soviet
26 May 1990	Formation of Democratic Movement of Kyrgyzstan
June 1990	Outbreak of intercommunal violence in southern regions
23 June 1990	Leaders of Central Asian states meet in Bishkek
28 October 1990	Askar Akaev elected president of Kyrgyzstan
5 February 1991	Name of the capital changed from Frunze to Bishkek
13 October 1991	Akaev elected president unopposed with 95% of the vote
5 May 1993	Parliament adopts new constitution
10 May 1993	Kyrgyzstan leaves the rouble zone
14 December 1993	Apas Jumagalov becomes prime minister
30 January 1994	Referendum on support for the president
June 1994	Round table conference on 'Russians in Kyrgyzstan'
August 1994	Closure of parliamentary paper *Svobodny gory*
September 1994	Dissolution of parliament
22 October 1994	Referendum on constitutional change
5 February 1995	First round of parliamentary elections
19 February 1995	Second round of elections
24 December 1995	Presidential election won by Akaev
10 February 1996	Constitutional referendum on extending presidential powers
September 1996	Meeting of state Security Council accuses senior officials of financial improprieties
January 1997	Trial of Topchubek Turgunaliev
May 1997	Sentencing of *Res Publika* journalists
July 1997	Muratbek Imanaliev replaces Roza Otunbaeva as foreign minister

PREFACE

Kyrgyzstan is a land of contradictions. Though part of Central Asia, its physical aspect is characterised by huge mountain ranges and plentiful water supplies rather than the dry desert sands and periodic drought of popular imagination. To the south west runs the Pamir-Alai range, whilst the north-eastern territories are dominated by the snow covered peaks of the Tian Shan mountains. Tucked into the far eastern tip of the country is Victory Peak reaching a height of 7,439 metres, and serving as a useful corrective to a Scottish based writer tempted to boast about the Highlands. These mountains, which have helped to create much of the mythology of Kyrgyz life, also serve to divide the country, with travel between the various regions dependent upon planes, trains through Uzbekistan or hair-raising road journeys via high mountain passes in the care of drivers with no concept of not over-taking on the bend regardless of the drop below.

These mountains, which bifurcate the country geographically, also create political divisions, in particular contributing to tensions between the north and south of the republic. Administratively Kyrgyzstan is made up of six regions: Talas, Chu, Issyk Kul, Naryn, Jalalabad and Osh. The north west is dominated by the Talas and Chu regions, bordering on southern Kazakhstan, whose rivers flow between the mountains, creating valleys with rich agricultural potential which also provide shepherds and their flocks with a refuge during the bitter winter months. Though undistinguished as a town, Talas is the legendary home of the epic hero Manas whose adventures have been recounted in yurts (felt tents) across the country for many decades and whose millennium was formally celebrated by the Kyrgyz state in 1995. Bishkek, the capital of the Chu region and of the republic, is a more attractive if slightly sleepy colonial town where traditional and Soviet architecture meet. Nestling below the mountains, its streets are watered by a network of aryks (irrigation ditches) which keep the air cool and feed the numerous trees which offer shade to the citizens in the heat of summer.

To the east of the Chu valley lies the Issyk Kul region, the approach to which was so vividly described by Eugene Schuyler following his travels through Central Asia in 1873:

Here the banks of the Tchu, as well as of the Kebin, are rocky and precipitous, and the river confined within a narrow space, rushes swiftly by, forming picturesque rapids and cataracts... The road crossed and recrossed the torrent, now passing on a cornice through a narrow defile, and again coming out on an open valley, where the stream grew wider and shallower, and where were sometimes small green meadows and clumps of willow... The scenery was certainly very grand, but owed its beauty entirely to the mass of bare rock, and to the contrasts in colour observable, some being of a rich reddish purple sandstone conglomerate, and others of black trap with occasional patches of yellow, grey and brown.[1]

The traveller taking this route today will find that little has changed, as he or she approaches the 170 km long Lake Issyl Kul, whose northern side attracts so many tourists from the territories of the former Soviet Union and beyond. Though in parts spoilt by concrete sanatoria and the other consequences of tourism, many of the surrounding valleys remain virtually untouched by modernity. Even wilder are the less favoured southern shores, whose inhabitants face a constant struggle for survival against the forces of nature. This was evident in the autumn of 1997, when one group of villagers sought to cull a growing wolf population that was threatening their livestock. The capital of this region is Karakol (Przeval'sk under the Russians), a town where many Russians have chosen to stay and which is famous for its apple groves and poplar trees.

At the centre of the country lies the Naryn region, home territory of Turdakun Usubaliev, Communist Party first secretary from the early 1960s to the mid-1980s. Much of this territory which borders on China is inhospitable mountain land, bitterly cold in winter and unbearably hot during the summer. Here semi-nomadic farmers scratch out a living under the sharp blue skies on which so many travellers have commented. In the spring and summer they load their yurts onto camels, horses or trucks, and lead their flocks to mountain pastures. Here, as they guard their flocks from predators, the men talk, drink kumiss (fermented mare's milk), and develop the almost instinctive relationship with their chestnut horses so tenderly sketched in Chingiz Aitmatov's story 'Farewell Gyulsary'. In this region, made up almost entirely of ethnic Kyrgyz, young boys of eight and old men of eighty ride their steeds with surety and arrogance, leaving the women at home to carry out domestic and agricultural chores.

In recent decades it is these four regions that have tended to dominate political life in the country, with many key appointments during the Soviet era and afterwards going to political families from these areas. By way of contrast the two southern regions, dominated by the fertile lands of the Fergana valley, have seen themselves as poor relations, lacking in political influence and economically impoverished. Ethnically they differ in having only a tiny minority of Slavs and Europeans, most of whom live in the north of the country, and instead having a substantial Uzbek population whose presence reinforces the 'oriental' ambience of the region. In the towns of Osh, Jalalabad, and the surrounding villages the influence of Islam is more pervasive, evident in the more insistent calls to prayer from newly built minarets and the occasional appearance of women in veils.

These geographical and cultural differences are reinforced by a variety of lifestyles, though recent decades have witnessed some degree of homogenisation. In the larger towns modern housing and apartment blocks co-exist with more traditional courtyard centred homes, whilst Bishkek, Osh and other cities have seen the emergence of small shanty towns created by rural dwellers seeking a better life in the cities. Outside the urban areas families live in smaller homes, often comprising a gated courtyard, surrounded on one side by living accomodation, on a second by a building for cooking and storage, and on the third a stable where flocks can be protected from the rigours of winter. And for those who take the flocks up to pasture, the most basic shelter is provided by the felt yurt or the less elegant modern canvas tent which has often replaced it.

Within their homes the inhabitants of Kyrgyzstan live in different ways, in part determined by ethnicity. In Bishkek, where Russians continue to make up a sizeable proportion of the population, the typical family is small and the diet combines Eastern and Slavic tastes: black bread and flat nans, fruit and salad, mutton, served in the north with tea or vodka. Amongst the ethnic Kyrgyz, families are larger, with the number of children born per thousand residents in 1996 running at 27.7 for the Kyrgyz population as against 8.5 for the Russians. Outside of the large cities Kyrgyz diet and lifestyles are more distinctive, with the basic diet consisting of bread, salad and fresh fruit, a noodle and mutton dish known as laghman, and various types of meat for those who can afford it. And when a guest arrives in a country home it would be usual for an animal to be slaughtered, and the guest to be offered the best parts of the sheep, including its head and eyes, or the somewhat tastier stuffed goat's stomach, filled with onions, spices and meat. Then in the south of the country Uzbek influences also in evidence in the taste for plov, a dish combining rice, spices and mutton.

These geographical, political and cultural divisions remind us that this is a country of considerable ethnic and religious variation, where, at the point of independence, the titular nationality made up just over half the population. In the summer of 1990 the southern regions witnessed bloody intercommunal violence, in which over 300 people died, and these killings left a legacy of tension between the Kyrgyz and Uzbek communities of the Fergana Valley. For all this, and despite minority fears, there has so far been no repetition of these tragic events. Many communities remain dissatisfied, as is evident from the substantial emigration of Slavs and Europeans, but overt conflict has been avoided. Equally important, the burgeoning social role of religion has not translated into any substantial support for Islamicist political visions amongst significant sections of the population. In the south more women have adopted Muslim dress codes and the number of mosques and medressahs has grown considerably, but most of the Kyrgyz remain wary of more radical religious manifestations, preferring not to abandon their partial acceptance of women in public life, alcohol or extravagant burial plots. More problematic may be socio-economic and cultural differences in a country where rural life has changed little over the centuries yet where the younger generation of the capital speak the language of the market and the ballot box. In the major cities there has emerged a small class of 'new rich' whose lifestyle contrasts sharply with that of substantial sections of the population for whom independence has been marked by a rapid fall in living standards and, in many cases, real poverty.

* * * *

This book offers an introduction to this fascinating little country where Western forms meet Central Asian traditions. In the first chapter I offer an overview of Kyrgyz history until the collapse of the USSR, pointing to some of the key developments that have created the modern state, and noting the contribution that the nomadic tradition may have made to the more pluralistic nature of Kyrgyz society. In the second and largest chapter I look at political developments, examining the structures created after 1991, the development of social and political organisations, the key role played by President Akaev, and the attempts that have been made to preserve ethnic and religious peace. Here I also stress the importance of informal politics rooted in kinship and geographical connections, though the precise political salience of these is difficult to assess with any accuracy. Towards the end of this chapter I note various recent developments that undermine the republic's image as an 'island of democracy', though it should be born in mind that, within the context of Central Asian authoritarianism, the four and a half million people of Kyrgyzstan enjoy a greater degree of freedom than most of those around them.

Freedom is all very well, but independence has led to economic impoverishment for many of the population, with a small minority reaping great benefits whilst the vast majority exist close to, or below, the breadline. Kyrgyzstan's problems are exacerbated by the fact that despite the presence of substantial gold reserves, the republic lacks the massive energy and mineral resources of its immediate neighbours and, with the possible exception of Tajikistan, remains one of the least accessible of the former Soviet republics. The final chapter examines some of the ways in which this tiny republic has sought to ensure stability at home and guarantee some degree of security so that it can preserve its independence. To this end it has sought new alliances in the wider world though these have not been sufficient to free it from its long term dependence upon Russia and other successor states. In a book of this size some issues can only be dealt with in an abbreviated fashion, and simplifications are inevitable. Nonetheless, it is hoped that readers will find this a useful introduction and one that will encourage them to pursue further their interests—whether intellectual, commercial or tourist—in this most attractive of countries.

Inevitably the writing of a book of this type would have been impossible without the help and support of many people. In particular I would like to thank the Nuffield Foundation whose financial support for a project on civil society made possible a research visit to Kyrgyzstan during which useful material was gathered for this book. In Bishkek, valuable help was provided by the Kyrgyz Peace Research Centre, and much was learned from conversations with Altyrkul Alisheva, Syrgak Salmorbekov, Zumrat Salmorbekova, Dina Shukhurova and the centre's director Anara Tabyshalieva. Thanks are also due to Medetbek Sultanbaev who shared both thoughts and materials which greatly enriched my understanding of Kyrgyzstan, and to Natalia Kigai who provided valuable research assistance. In addition I would like to thank the various government officials, journalists and social activists who made themselves available and answered my numerous questions. As is so often the case, much was learnt within the less formal context of daily life—in cafes, on buses and in the street. Special thanks must go to Sasha, a party official turned taxi driver in the Issyk Kul region; also to the semi-nomadic farmers of the Koch-Korka district of the Naryn region who for several days overwhelmed me with their hospitality, accustomed a rather squeamish Westerner to having his dinner killed in front of him, taught me that kumiss and vodka do not mix and, more importantly, reminded me that outside of Bishkek the concepts and categories of Western political science have little resonance. Thanks should also go to the reviewer of the draft manuscript, to the editorial staff of Harwood Academic Publishers for their helpful editorial comments, and to all those who have written on Central Asia and Kyrgyzstan, in particular Eugene Huskey, Guy Imart, Bruce Pannier and Ian Pryde, some of whose essays are cited in the references and the section on further reading. Needless to say, none of these should be blamed for any errors of fact or judgement. Finally, special thanks as always to Jill, Joseph and Caitlin who not for the first time have had to put up with an absent husband and father, yet who still offer constant love and encouragement and occasionally prove willing to wear the unusual hats with which he returns.

NB. In the preparation of this manuscript I have made considerable use of the Russian language media from the republic but, in accordance with the publisher's wishes, have attempted to keep notes minimal.

1   E. Schuyler, *Turkistan* (London, Routledge and Kegan Paul, 1966), p. 256

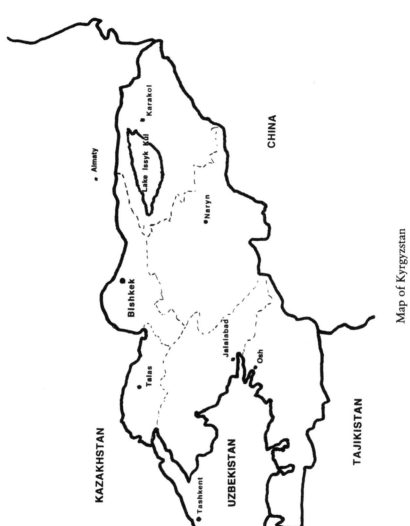

Map of Kyrgyzstan

Chapter 1

FROM NOMADS TO CITIZENS:
THE GENESIS OF INDEPENDENT STATEHOOD

BEFORE THE RUSSIANS

The territory that we now know as Kyrgyzstan was inhabited long before the arrival of the Kyrgyz. Archaeologists have found evidence of settlements from the Paleolithic period, and of the development of ironworking and more complex social structures by the 7th century BC. Amongst the more significant occupants of the region were the Scythian tribes who offered such bitter resistance to Alexander the Great's onslaught on Central Asia. For much of the first Christian millennium, the region was the site of numerous conflicts as various tribal groupings established their dominance for a while and then fell apart. From the 6th century onwards the dominant forces were Turkic, though the struggle between different tribes and attacks from China often rendered life precarious for the ordinary inhabitant of the region whose livelihood was undermined by constant warfare. From the 10th to the 12th century the region came under the control of the Turkic Qarakhanids who ruled from the Chu valley area, crossing contemporary Kazakhstan and Kyrgyzstan, and established bases at Uzgen in the southern part of the country and Buran in the north where little remains but an impressively restored minaret. During their period of dominance the Qarakhanids devoted some attention to the Islamicisation of Central Asia, though most of the peoples on this eastern fringe appeared reluctant to give up their traditional customs and ways of life.

Throughout this period it is impossible to find more than passing reference to a people known as the Kyrgyz, and their origins remain the subject of controversy.[1] Some of their forerunners appear to have lived on the banks of the Upper Yenisey river in Siberia until the 10th century—though some have claimed that these groups had originally emigrated from Central Asia. They in turn were gradually forced to emigrate southwards under pressure from various tribal confederations and then from the Mongol advances. Settling in the Tien Shan region they were unable to escape Mongol domination, and during the 13th century found themselves in the territory of Chingiz Khan's second son Chagatai. As imperial power declined during the 15th century the various Kyrgyz tribes, themselves the product of a mixture of the people of the region and various incoming Mongol and Turkic groups, appear to have created the first independent khanate with some degree of autonomy from nominal Mongol overlords. According to Soviet historians, it was during this period that the Kyrgyz developed a distinctive language, and acquired a sense of nationhood, though social organisation remained centred around tribal and kinship ties. For all this, they faced an uphill struggle to maintain their freedom against the Mongol Oirats and during the 17th century many Kyrgyz groups were forced to move, whether to the Fergana valley region, or further south to what today is northern Tajikistan, or to eastern Turkestan, now part of China.

By this time Kyrgyz society had developed around a distinctive, if flexible, political-administrative structure, based upon independent family and tribal associations, and rooted in the nomadic lifestyles of the people. Communities were organised around kinship groups and every Kyrgyz was supposed to be able to trace their ancestors back at least seven generations—an ability increasingly lost in the modern cities of Kyrgyzstan though not in the countryside. As families grew their auls (mobile villages) were split up, as sons left home with flocks and spouse to seek fresh pastures elsewhere. These were also an extremely mobile people, who packed up their tents and moved on once the grass had been exhausted by their flocks of sheep and goats. Life here revolved around the seasons and animals, as shepherds fought to delay lambing until the end of the winter, as women kept the home and prepared kumiss, and children gathered cattle dung to be dried for fuel.

Each family belonged to a larger clan group, and each of these in turn was part of a wider tribal confederation. And though these were mostly nomadic peoples each of these communities had a territorial base, and each was dominated by an 'aristocracy'—defined largely in terms of the size of cattleholdings which in turn determined levels of access to the most favourable pastures. At the same time tribal life was characterised by a degree of debate and consultation which would have been unthinkable in the settled oases to the west, with some contemporaries seeing the 'election' of khans and resolution of conflicts through discussion as underlying the more 'democratic' nature of Kyrgyz politics during the 1990s. There was also a considerable degree of flexibility in the selection of leaders, so that when traditionally dominant families failed to produce people of high calibre, communities would seek out men of ability from other leading families to exercise authority. Yet these 'democratic' aspects of tribal life should not be over-stated. Leadership tended to remain with certain families, though most Kyrgyz remained suspicious of strong authority figures, and for much of the year the individual aul governed its own life and activity. Only occasionally did communities come together, perhaps for wedding celebrations or for the great games, when Kyrgyz horsemen raced each other through the valleys or competed in the traditional alaman-baiga when the horsemen risked life and limb in competition for a goat's carcass.[2]

Each clan or tribal group developed its own myths about legendary ancestors and great events of the past. Typical of these, and since elevated into a national epic by Soviet scholars and contemporary nationalists, was the story of Manas. Traditionally passed down from generation to generation in oral fashion, a written text was produced in the Soviet era which grew to several times the length of the *Odyssey*. The origins of the story are lost, despite the presence of a purported grave in the Talas region and the UNESCO sponsored 1,000 anniversary celebration of Manas held in 1995. Like other epics, Manas tells the story of a Kyrgyz hero and his exploits against the enemies of the people. In later versions this takes the form of a struggle of good Muslims versus wicked infidels, but the story is perhaps less interesting for its 'boys-own' exploits than for the many insights it gives into the life and customs of the Kyrgyz. And though the epic stressed the unity of the Kyrgyz, most of their history has been one of disunity and internal struggle, with regional and tribal groupings struggling for dominance rather than pooling sovereignty to combat much greater external menaces. During the Mongol invasions tribal infighting prevented any form of consistent struggle against those seen as 'barbarians' from the north, and in the 18th and 19th centuries there emerged the break between northern and southern tribal groups that continues to play a divisive role in Kyrgyz politics.

In the middle of the 18th century the Kyrgyz became subject to the Chinese who left their nomadic lifestyle largely untouched, but by the end of the century the much closer and increasingly powerful khanate of Kokand began to make its presence felt. First the southern and then the northern territories came under the khanate's control and by 1830 all of the Kyrgyz tribes were paying formal tribute. Under the influence of Kokand, Islam appears to have taken a deeper hold in Kyrgyz territory, especially in the southern regions where numerous mosques and medressahs sprang up. Yet even during this period many Kyrgyz remained unwilling to abandon their traditional customs and the religion that developed was highly syncretic, combining nominal allegiance to Islam with considerable faith in holy places, saints and evils spirits. In the northern territories, though most Kyrgyz called themselves Muslims, the influence of Islam remained limited and, rather ironically, it was to be the Russian invaders who helped to strengthen the institutional basis of Islam from the end of the 19th century onwards.[3] Though local leaders preserved most of their privileges under the new rulers, a perceived weakening of Kokand's power in the 1840s led to a series of rebellions in various parts of the region, notably in 1845 when the Osh Kyrgyz took advantage of the absence of the regular garrison to rebel against the harsh tax policies of the khanate. Further revolts took place in 1870–71, led by the remarkable Kurmanjan-datka, the widow of a Kyrgyz aristocrat who was for a while accepted as a leader by many of the mountain tribes. Such revolts, however, made little impact upon Kokand so long as it retained a strong international position, and in most cases such challenges proved little more than an irritant which could be put down relatively easily and with considerable brutality. Moreover, the khanate proved especially adept at divide and rule politics, which kept the Kyrgyz fighting each other and unable to break free from Kokand's dominance until the latter's position was undermined by the growing Russian presence in the region.[4]

UNDER THE RULE OF ST. PETERSBURG

Kyrgyz contacts with Russia date back to the beginning of the 17th century when Peter the Great's ambassador to the Jungar khanate, artillery captain Ivan Unkovsky, visited the region. Other Russians followed, especially from the late 18th century as adventurers, scholars and travellers began to penetrate Central Asia, some stimulated by intellectual curiosity and others by a desire to spread Russian influence or counter that of the English. A number of these published interesting travel books. I.G. Andreev (1743–1801) was the first to point to the importance of tribal structures; P.P. Semenov (1827–1914) and the Kazakh enlightener Chokan Valikhanov (1835–65) both offered valuable insights into Kyrgyz geography, history and social organisation. In 1775 the Chu valley Kyrgyz had sent their first embassy to St. Petersburg, though they were forced to wait nearly a year for an audience with Catherine the Great. At the beginning of the next century various delegations were sent to the Russian authorities in Siberia as Kyrgyz tribes, perhaps influenced by the Kazakh Greater Horde's decision to accept Russian suzerainty, sought protection against Kokand. As the latter's position declined the northern Kyrgyz sent numerous letters to the Siberian authorities appealing for help, and during the 1850s and 1860s a number of tribes declared their allegiance to the tsar. In 1862 Kyrgyz soldiers fought alongside Russians to take the fort of Pishpek (later Frunze and then Bishkek), and by the time the Kokand khanate was finally destroyed in 1876 all of the Kyrgyz had formally submitted to Russian rule.

The new Russian rulers initially proved satisfied with political dominance and interfered only to a limited extent in the day to day affairs of the Kyrgyz. Administratively Russian rule in Central Asia was marked by constant reorganisation, with the majority of the Kyrgyz territory in the first instance allocated to the Semirechie oblast (administrative region) within the Turkestan governor-generalship. From 1882–97 this region was transferred to the Steppe Administration, after which it returned to Turkestan's jurisdiction. During the same period the southerly regions were located within the Fergana and Syr darya regions, each of which was in turn divided into districts (uezdy). Through most of the pre-revolutionary period each region within Central Asia remained under military governors, but in the districts there emerged parallel Russian and local authority structures, with the new rulers relying on traditional elites to maintain order. This had the advantage of leaving unpopular decisions to be implemented by local leaders who then bore the brunt of popular displeasure.

Despite the hands-off policy favoured in the early years of Russian dominance, it was perhaps inevitable that these two very different cultures would clash as time progressed. In particular the newcomers' distinctive ideas about agriculture and land use were to provoke tensions as they sought to impose the principle of private ownership and settled farming on groups who relied heavily on nomadism, and viewed land as the property of all. Successive land statutes in 1867 and 1891 made the practice of nomadism problematic, especially as Russian settlers were given land in locations that often obstructed the age old pattern of cattle herding. From the 1860s onwards Russian and Ukrainian settlers trickled and then flooded into the northern territories, with an estimated 3,500 families having arrived by the early 1880s. From 1893, some also ventured further afield setting up small farms in the Fergana valley, though these were never to be as numerous as those in the north. Justifiable fear of Kyrgyz resentment, as well as the problems of agriculture where irrigation was poorly developed, led the authorities to curtail immigration from the mid-1890s, but after 1905 it resumed on a much larger scale.

Though Russian policies served to undermine traditional ways of life, agriculture, and in particular cattle breeding, remained the predominant occupation for the majority of the indigenous population. In the late 1890s, 85% of those in the Pishpek district were still nomadic or semi-nomadic. Crops began to spread as Russian settlers introduced cotton, rice, potatoes and tobacco, whilst in the Issyl Kul area Russian farmers successfully developed grain cultivation. Russian patterns of rural development also brought changes to Kyrgyz lifestyles, as the seizure of the best lands or obstruction of nomadic routes led to the impoverishment of many Kyrgyz families and increasing settlement of local communities. Over half were reported to be more or less settled farmers by 1917. There was also a very limited industrial development, though by 1913 only 1400 people were employed in such enterprises which were largely concerned with the processing of agricultural goods.

With this changing economic structure came the growth of urban centres, with Pishpek's population growing from around 2,000 in 1882 to over 15,000 by 1913, of whom nearly two-thirds were Russian. Other towns exhibited similar levels of growth. Yet urbanisation largely excluded the Kyrgyz who remained firmly located in the countryside, with the towns largely inhabited by Russian professionals or Tatar traders.

For all these changes, one can find little evidence of overt revolt during the early period, with such incidents as took place confined to the refusal to pay taxes, rejection of official candidates in local elections and the occasional murder of hated landlords. Moreover, most of these were directed against indigenous officials put in position by the Russian administrators. There were few public protests, though the great reciter Toktogul Saltylganov (1864–1933) was singled out by Soviet scholars for songs which denounced the rich and aspired to social justice. Accused of participation in the 1898 Andizhan uprising which saw Islamic slogans used in an effort to drive out the Russian conquerors, Saltylganov was condemned to death, but his sentence was later commuted to seven years of Siberian exile. More peaceful were efforts to bring education to the local population, with Muslim reformers (jadids) seeking to establish a network of schools across Central Asia that would combine respect for tradition with openness to modern learning. A few were opened in Kyrgyz towns, including in 1914 one for women, but these brave enlightenment efforts, which were treated with suspicion by colonial authorities and conservative mullahs alike, had a very limited impact.

During the first years of the century, revolutionary circles began to develop in a number of Central Asian cities, in part as a result of St. Petersburg's ill considered policy of exiling political activists to the regions. In early 1904, V. Loitsev, a Marxist active in Pishpek, was sentenced to five years for spreading revolutionary literature, but in general such activity was even more limited here than in other parts of Central Asia and largely confined to a few intellectuals and soldiers. During the 1905 revolution there were some public meetings and a few strikes, notably of oil and postal workers, but these were largely confined to Slavic personnel and on the whole Kyrgyz peasants remained unaffected. Following the collapse of the revolution martial law was imposed in the Semirechie and Fergana regions, and political power was more firmly placed in the hands of the police and the military. Political activists were rounded up and social-democratic circles destroyed, though in subsequent years there were sporadic attempts to re-establish revolutionary groups in Pishpek. For example, in the spring of 1911 a new circle was created by I.S.Svinukhov, a recently released political prisoner, who sought to bring together local workers and craftsmen, whilst similar groups sprung up in other cities. Yet, despite the efforts of later Soviet historians to magnify the significance of such groups, their political impact was marginal.

Nonetheless official reports suggest increasing alarm at the anti-government mood of certain sections of the population in the years before the outbreak of the First World War. Indigenous farmers protested land seizures or tax burdens, whilst new settlers were increasingly critical of the administration. The privations of wartime only increased resentment as prices rose, shortages increased, and the sons of some Russian settlers were drafted into the army. Initially the local population was excluded from military service, but attempts to mobilise them in support of the war effort in June 1916 led to a mass rebellion across Central Asia. Even though the mobilisation decree spoke of drafting men into work in the rear of the Russian armed forces, many were unhappy about being drawn into a war in which one of the enemies was Turkey, guardian of the holy places of Islam. More importantly the revolt reflected deep seated grievances that had been building up over previous years as Kyrgyz farmers and nomads were gradually impoverished by excessive demands and Russian setlement.

In mid-July some 10,000 people gathered in Osh chanting 'we will not fight' and 'we will not give our sons', and by August the revolt had reached the northern areas where the more perceptive noted that in Semirechie the list of those being mobilised excluded the sons of the rich. Violence bred violence as Russian settlers backed by the army used the revolt as an excuse to seize more land and, though it was often Kyrgyz officials who bore the brunt of the violence, the rebellion was accompanied by brutal attacks on more isolated Russian settlements with over 2,000 dying in this region alone. Yet the rebels were unable to resist the Russian army and by November the revolt had petered out in most of the region. Russian forces burnt down Kyrgyz settlements and around a third of the Kyrgyz population fled to China. In addition to the disastrous human consequences, with around 100,000 Kyrgyz deaths, the revolt had major economic consequences as rural labour forces were depleted by population loss and conscription, and during 1916–17 sowing and output of most crops fell dramatically. All these factors only added to the tense relationships between Russians and Kyrgyz and fed into the revolutionary fervour of 1917.[5]

THE ESTABLISHMENT OF SOVIET POWER, 1917–28

Following the outbreak of revolution in Russia, the first soviets of workers' deputies appeared in the Kyrgyz regions in March 1917, initially in the southern town of Kyzyl-Kiia and a number of mining settlements, and then in Pishpek, Tokmak, Przeval'sk, Naryn and Osh. Though there were few representatives of the indigenous nationalities on these bodies and only a minority of their members were radical socialists, they soon found themselves at odds with those authorities loyal to the provisional government. Alongside the soviets there also emerged a number of Muslim organisations of which the most influential appears to have been the Kyrgyz revolutionary-democratic union 'Bukhara' which was formed in May 1917 and within several months claimed 7,000 members. The aim of this organisation, whose agenda appears to have become increasingly radical—which may account for the key place it occupies in some Soviet histories—was to advance the demands of the poorest sections of the population. In this they were supported by the various trade union organisations that sprung up in the mining, oil and handicraft industries whose proclamations usually combined political and economic demands including an end to war, the redistribution of land, and government efforts to combat hunger and poverty.

In the months immediately following the fall of tsarism the territory of Kyrgyzstan experienced considerable economic decline, in part resulting from the breakdown of production but further exacerbated by the return to the country of thousands who had fled during the 1916 revolt. This was the situation the Bolsheviks inherited when they seized power in St. Petersburg and Moscow, though it was to be some time before they gained complete control of Central Asia. There was still no separate Bolshevik organisation. In the Kyrgyz territories, at the time of the second revolution and in the following months, it was to prove difficult to create coherent socialist groupings amidst the ebb and flow of civil war. Only in December was Soviet power formally established in northern Talas region, and it was to take a further six months before nominal Bolshevik control was established in much of the country. And even then real mastery of the region was to require considerable political and military struggle over the next two years. Establishing a proper administrative power was to prove equally difficult, for amongst the local population only representatives of the landowning classes and clergy could read, whilst amongst the Slavic population colonial attitudes still prevailed.

The problems of the new regime were further exacerbated by the resistance of the basmachi—bandits or popular heroes depending upon one's perspective—who enjoyed considerable popular support in the southern regions of the country and virtually controlled the Fergana valley for a while. In late 1919 armed bands were able to take over Osh, Jalalabad and Naryn, but gradually they were pushed back, in part defeated by internal squabbles and in part by the Bolsheviks' skilful combination of carrot and stick. In the summer of 1919 Mikhail Frunze, who had spent some of his previous career in the region, was sent to lead the Red Army in Central Asia. He proved not only a capable military commander but also someone who understood the sort of concessions that might win over a local population weary of revolution and war. Together with the newly created Turkestan Commission created by the Bolsheviks, Frunze brought the terror to an end and made it clear that the Bolsheviks would come to some form of accomodation with traditional ways of life. Under such circumstances the basmachi campaign gradually weakened and its more militant leaders eventually gave themselves up or fled into exile. After 1920 there was no serious challenge to Soviet power in Kyrgyzstan until the late 1980s.

In April 1918 the territory of the Kyrgyz was included in the new Turkestan Autonomous Soviet Socialist Republic within the Russian Federation (RSFSR). Initially the Bolsheviks appeared to accept the pre-revolutionary understanding of the Kyrgyz as a distinctive tribal grouping within the Kazakh (then known as Kyrgyz) community, and in consequence referred to them as the Kara-Kyrgyz. In the early 1920s there was considerable discussion of the administrative and territorial structures to be devised for the new state, with considerable debate as to whether the region we now know as Kyrgyzstan should be included in Turkestan, Kazakhstan or the Russian Federation. During the national demarcation of 1924, subordination to Russia won the day, with the area becoming the Kara-Kyrgyz Autonomous Oblast.[6] Further titular changes took place in 1925 and 1927, and then in 1936 the republic acquired the formal title of the Kyrgyz Soviet Socialist Republic, and thus became one of the constituent units of the Soviet Union.

Though by 1936 the promise of republican autonomy had been rendered largely meaningless by Stalin's ruthless centralisation drive, the constant administrative reorganisations after 1924 had a significant impact upon future developments. On the positive side they created an embryonic state structure whose ranks were to be gradually filled by a new elite educated within the Soviet framework, thus ensuring that when the USSR collapsed there was something for the newly independent country to build upon. Less happily, the national demarcation, in seeking to combine both ethnic principles and economic rationality, created the basis for the conflicts that were to emerge under Gorbachev and after. In particular, the division of the Fergana Valley in the south left sizeable Uzbek communities—whose numbers would grow still further as a result of administrative tinkering in 1936—stranded in the Kyrgyz part of the region.

Creating administrative structures was all very well, but the new Soviet authorities faced the task of making a reality of their power in a country impoverished by war and revolution, suspicious of the intentions of the new

masters and lacking any real popular commitment to the socialism proclaimed by the Bolsheviks. The task was complicated by the insufficient
number of ethnic Kyrgyz personnel and the reliance on Slavic cadres. Though
a 1924 law required the translation of laws into Kyrgyz, and the leading
bodies of the party organisation were dominated numerically by Kyrgyz, in
practice decision making remained in the hands of Russians, Ukrainians,
Tatars and Jews. Nonetheless, some effort was made to improve the
educational opportunities open to the Kyrgyz with a variety of courses made
available to would-be administrators and party leaders. Thus trained, considerable numbers were promoted to key positions in the late 1920s, though
there were many complaints that the efficiency of native cadres was undermined by the impact of tribalism and family connections which led to the
dominance of 'groupism' and cronyism in public life. Efforts to encourage
the Kyrgyz to join the party and administration continued and were reinforced by promises of full indigenization of the apparatus by 1934.

Administrative change was accompanied by social and cultural change,
though as elsewhere in Central Asia during the early 1920s the authorities
were careful in their struggle with remnants of the old way of life. Early com-
mitments included a promise of equality for men and women, the prohibi-
tion of some traditional marriage customs and education for all, though in
the event rhetoric inevitably surpassed the reality. Despite the long-term
commitment to reducing the public role of religion, the early 1920s were
marked by a cautious approach to Islam in Central Asia, with religious schools
and courts allowed to function until around 1926–27 and, not infrequently,
religious leaders coopted into local administration. Only the most resolutely
anti-Soviet mullahs were repressed, but in predominantly rural Kyrgyzstan
the drive to win over the population, as well as the practical limitations
imposed by the absence of personnel in the villages, took priority over ideological orthodoxy, and not until the late 1920s were serious efforts launched
to eradicate the remnants of the old and impose a new Soviet culture.

All these efforts at administrative and cultural change were undermined by
the dire economic state of the country in the early 1920s. Following the 1916
revolt, revolution and civil war, the economy lay in ruins, with the sown area
reduced by nearly half and livestock herds at a third of pre-1916 levels. In the
years after the establishment of Soviet power official policies focused on land
reform, which gave several thousand landless peasants small holdings,
though in the southern regions continued resistance and limited administrative penetration meant that land redistribution could not really begin until
the late 1920s. Simultaneously some effort was made to reduce further the
importance of nomadism to the local economy, though it was to require the

brutality of the 1930s to persuade many former nomads of the virtues of settled agriculture. By the late 1920s official figures claimed that economic production and livestock herds had reached their pre-war levels, though some of these gains were to be undermined by the collectivisation programmes launched at the end of the decade.

STALINISM IN KYRGYZSTAN

The triumph of Stalin, following the political struggles of the 1920s, meant that Kyrgyzstan would not escape the consequences of the new policies launched at the end of that decade and the beginning of the next. In the economic sphere the campaigns for industrialisation and collectivisation had a major impact. New industries sprang up, especially in the northern regions, and the hydro-electric potential of this mountainous region began to be developed. Amongst the new industries created or expanded during this period were metal working, textiles, sugar refining and meatpacking, and by 1937 over 200 large scale industrial enterprises had been created. Considerable work also went into the creation of a social infrastructure, with the development of new settlements and homes, the building of hundreds of schools and hospitals, and huge expenditure on the expansion of irrigation networks. Some effort was also made to exploit mineral and energy resources, and by 1940 Kyrgyzstan was producing around 40% of all the coal produced in Central Asia (excluding Kazakhstan). As a result of these efforts, official statistics reported that in the period 1913–40 gross industrial output had risen 9.9 times.

In the predominantly rural sector of the economy, official sources described collectivisation as having 'solved' the problem of transition from nomadic to settled agriculture, and by 1940 98% of the republic's farmers found themselves in collective farms. In practice, however, the results of collectivisation were of doubtful benefit to the ordinary peasant who, as elsewhere in the Soviet Union, offered mostly sullen resistance. This was most evident in the declining size of livestock herds—with the number of sheep and goats falling from 3.1 million in 1924 to just under 1 million by 1932, and the number of horses from 660,000 to 494,00—with the levels of the late 1920s not to be achieved again until the 1950s or even later. Suspicious of the collective farms and believing that they represented a device to confiscate their cattle, many peasants simply consumed their flocks, whether as an act of resistance or because they were unable to get adequate supplies of fodder from the new rural authorities.

This campaign often served to create tensions in the countryside, as village communities and even families divided as how best to respond. Tananbai, the human hero of Chingiz Aitmatov's story 'Farewell Gyulsary', recalls how during his first enthusiasm for the new socialist system he had played a role in the denunciation of his half brother as a 'kulak', telling the party meeting that he 'wouldn't spare my own father to protect Soviet power'. In consequence his brother had spent seven years in Siberia and many in the village had turned against Tananbai.[7] Such events were not untypical, and those who resisted were often subject to heavy penalties, especially individuals described as 'rich peasants' who had their herds confiscated, were deprived of their electoral rights, and were sometimes imprisoned or assigned to forced labour on new industrial projects or the development of the Chu river for irrigation purposes. Others died in the mass famine of 1932, whilst those like prime minister Yusup Abdrakhmanov, who sought to divert grain to the starving, were deprived of their jobs and several years later shot for alleged 'anti-Soviet' activities.

Yet collectivisation may have had a less devastating effect in Central Asia than in other parts of the Soviet Union because traditional communities were not so effectively broken up. In 'Jamila', one of Aitmatov's earliest stories, the narrator recalls how various generations of the family had lived together over many years:

> It had been so since the time our people had been nomads, when our great-grandfathers used to break camp and round up their cattle together. We kept this tradition alive. When our village was collectivised, our fathers built their houses side by side. Actually we were all fellow-tribesmen—the whole of Aralskaya Street, stretching the length of the village to the river, was inhabited by our kins-folk.[8]

In consequence collective farms often represented a simple restructuring of existing kinship groups whilst leaving many traditional authority structures and agricultural practices in place.

From the late 1920s onwards religious and other traditional customs also came under attack. In March 1927 the khudzhum (advance) was launched in Central Asia. This was a mass propagandistic effort to encourage the liberation of women. Local authorities encouraged the public burning of the veil though in the southern town of Osh the veils were thrown off on the day announced by the authorities and then promptly put back on the next day by women under pressure from their families.[9] In practice, however, such measures were often counter-productive in that they could be portrayed as insensitive attacks on local tradition, whilst women active in the campaign were often subject to beatings and sometimes murder.

From around 1929 the campaign against religion increased in intensity, as mosques were closed, religious education prohibited, and religious activists subjected to repression. This campaign fell most heavily on the southern regions around the Fergana valley where Islam was much stronger and where the old ways of life retained their influence. Though the anti-religious campaign abated with the outbreak of war, and some mosques were later re-opened, the Stalinist state continued its efforts to reduce the impact of religion on everyday life. With regard to formal allegiance to Islam and dogmatic beliefs, it succeeded to some extent, especially in the Slavic dominated north where orthodox religion had never been strong, though many traditional customs such as circumcision and separate burial remained prevalent. But in the south successive attempts to break traditional habits often proved shortlived. Most notable here was the custom of making pilgrimage to the Throne of Suleiman on the outskirts of Osh, a habit which intensified during the Soviet period as an alternative to making the haj to Mecca. Despite fatwas from the officially recognised Muslim establishment condemning the practice as superstitious rather than Islamic, and despite repeated official campaigns against the site under both Stalin, and then during Khrushchev's renewed anti-religious campaign, people continued to flock there seeking spiritual solace or cures for their ills.[10]

In the political sphere, the Stalin years were most notable for the pervasive atmosphere of purge and terror. During the 1920s Moscow had attempted to maintain some degree of ethnic representation in party and administrative organisation, but from the early 1930s, as Stalin sought to ensure central control over the republics, considerations of efficiency and loyalty took priority over 'affirmative action'. Various purges had swept the Kyrgyz party organisation during the 1920s but these were largely administrative affairs connected to political struggles in the centre. From the early 1930s, however, purges began to take on a more sinister turn as the secret police discovered 'counter-revolutionary' cells in the Kyrgyz branch of the state planning agency and various intellectuals were accused of 'bourgeois-kulak nationalism'. A renewed purge of party ranks was launched in late 1933 which over the course of two years reduced membership of the Kyrgyz party from 19,932 to 6,385. As elsewhere in the USSR, the murder of the Leningrad party boss Sergei Kirov in December 1934 heralded far more thorough going purges in Kyrgyzstan, though by this time a number of leading figures had already been removed from their positions accused of nationalist deviations or even counter-revolutionary activities. Amongst the victims were Abdulkerim Sydykov, a leading economic planner, Yusup Abdrakhmanov, formerly chairman of the Kyrgyz Council of Peoples' Commissars, Kasym Tynstanov, a leading reformer and educationalist who had been Commissar of Education for much of the early Soviet period, and Torekul Aitmatov, the father of contemporary novelist Chingiz Aitmatov. The last three of these were rounded up in the affair of the 'Social-Turan' (or Turkic) party, guilty, according to the security services, of a variety of sins including nationalism, terrorism, anti-Soviet agitation and connections with right wing Trotskyites. Even now it is unclear whether this party actually existed or was a creation of the police, but its alleged leading members were arrested and brought before the courts. Found guilty on all counts, a total of 138 'conspirators' were shot and buried in a local sports centre during November 1938. Many others disappeared into the camps and execution cellars, or had their lives ruined as a result of kinship or friendship with 'enemies of the people', a category which included 63 people from the 72 member Central Commitee. Though there does appear to have been some resistance, evident in the creation of a central committee commission to investigate the activities of security services, their activities were to no avail, and most of the commission's members disappeared into the maelstrom.[11]

The Second World War, known in the USSR as the Great Patriotic War, brought an end to terror and saw the Kyrgyz economy boosted as more than thirty factories were evacuated eastwards to avoid capture by the Nazis. With them came skilled Slavic personnel, a number of Comintern orphans (including the son of Antonio Gramsci), as well as over 20,000 Poles who fell into Soviet hands as a result of the Molotov-Ribbentrop pact, and Soviet Germans whose loyalty was deemed suspect. Despite the ravages of the purges, Kyrgyz battalions fought hard against the invaders, with the Panfilov division playing a key role in the defence of Moscow. Though many Kyrgyz troops died needlessly as cavalry were sent against tanks, a few survived to join the triumphant march into Germany at the end of the war. On the domestic front life remained difficult, as women, old people and children were drafted in to maintain economic life, a role they continued to perform in many communities during the immediate post-war years when their menfolk failed to return.

FROM KHRUSHCHEV TO CHERNENKO

The death of Stalin in March 1953 led to some easing of central pressure, with Khrushchev allowing a partial de-Stalinisation and the rehabilitation of a few of those purged in the 1930s. Within the Kyrgyz Communist Party the proportion of indigenous members grew slowly, but only about a third of leading positions were occupied by Kyrgyz until the 1970s. Yet despite the Slavic dominance of leading economic and security positions, the Kyrgyz very cautiously began to assert themselves, especially in day-to-day politics. At the grass roots and in the rural areas where most Kyrgyz still lived, regional cliques or patronage networks remained. After 1945 considerable effort went into increasing the Kyrgyz membership of the party, though this numerical increase could not guarantee the political reliability of the new intake. A decree issued by the Communist Party Central Committee in 1958 criticised cadre policy in Kyrgyzstan, noting the failure of economic management by local personnel but, more importantly for our purposes, pointing to the ways in which traditional practices continued to dominate. Hence it attacked the failure to promote women, and the willingness of many officials to compromise with 'private property tendencies' and 'survivals of the past in everyday life': a semi-coded reference to the continued strength of religious practices.[12]

This partial re-assertion took place under the leadership of Turdakun Usubaliev, first secretary of the Kyrgyz Communist Party from 1961–86. Under his leadership, and indeed that of many of his Central Asian contemporaries, there developed a multifaceted approach to public life. On the one hand this entailed extreme obsequiousness, evident in public utterances about eternal friendship with the Russian older brother, and praise for the achievements of the Russian people and language. At the same time Usubaliev made increasing economic demands on Moscow for greater investment within the republic, and sought gradually to expand the number of positions available to indigenous elites. At one level this latter trend was highly discriminatory, because it meant allowing the Kyrgyz to dominate in part by simply increasing the total size of the administrative apparatus by around 150%, with most of the new posts occupied by members of the titular nationality. This policy was pushed through even in parts of the south where there were substantial Uzbek populations, a development that was to contribute to the bloody clashes of 1990.

Though this personnel policy represented a more overt reversion to clientelism, it was one which exhibited elements of change or adaptation as well as continuity. In consequence patronage networks would continue to be based upon kinship and regional identities, yet simultaneously the system allowed for the cooption of individuals from other groups, with even Slavs and Europeans drawn in on occasions. To more nationalistically minded Kyrgyz, Usubaliev's strategy was excessively compromised, entailing in particular a subservience towards Russia that was likely to end in the destruction of the Kyrgyz language and the emasculation of national culture. They also pointed out that the republican party leadership showed little initiative in dealing with, or even understanding, the growing socio-economic crisis in part stemming from the rapid rise in the rural population. Yet during Brezhnev's time in office the trends promoted by Usubaliev were strengthened because

Moscow appeared content to allow the creation of regional fiefdoms so long as political loyalty was maintained and five year plan targets more or less met.

Inevitably however, such autonomy could only be maintained through practices that were less than ideal from Moscow's perspective and which, in many respects, undermined Soviet rule. With weak central control, official policies could be distorted through processes that Andropov and Gorbachev were to describe as corrupt, with the 1970s and 1980s witnessing a rapid de facto expansion of the private sector in agriculture, often at the expense of collective and state farms. Such practices were generally left to flourish by the local authorities, as in the Osh oblast where private citizens often had much larger cattle herds than the state farms. Indeed, the inefficiency of parts of the state sector rendered such practices necessary if a population which grew by half a million in the 1980s was to be fed. Bending the rules was also common in the industrial sector, for despite the opening of many new enterprises in the post-war years and a national income that was reported to have grown by 300% in the years 1965–85, by the end of that period growth was slowing. Though still managing to report higher growth rates in the early 1980s than the USSR as a whole, these rates were still only half those of the 1960s and probably less than officially reported. At the same time it was becoming increasingly clear to both central planners and to more perceptive local officials that further substantial investment in the region was unlikely. Moreover, considerable growth rates disguised the fact that Kyrgyzstan was the second poorest republic within the USSR in 1979, with a per capita income around two-thirds of the Soviet average.

Growing regional indifference to central policies was also evident in other areas. From the late 1970s Moscow, under the influence of developments in Iran and Afghanistan, expressed increasing concern about the possible impact of Islamic revival upon its own Muslim subjects. Anti-Islamic propaganda was stepped up in response to central demands and an increasing number of press articles attacked the tendency of many party leaders at the local level to ignore the religious issue. Special attention was paid to the importance of such work in the Osh region where women were said to be especially inclined to popular superstition and young men susceptible to false claims about the innate links between religion and national belonging. Yet such campaigns had a largely formal appearance, seeking to show Moscow that work was being done in this area whilst having little impact upon public behaviour.

A far greater impact upon the everyday life of the Kyrgyz, especially those in the cities, came from the growing Russification of cultural life under

Usubaliev, with the language issue of particular concern to many Kyrgyz intellectuals. The Soviet era had witnessed script changes throughout Central Asia—from Arabic to Latin and then to Cyrillic—and the importation of many Russian loan words into local languages. At the same time Russian increasingly became the lingua franca in the cities, with the capital Frunze having few schools that taught in Kyrgyz. In consequence most Kyrgyz brought up after the war knew Russian better than their own language and were in danger of losing their sense of national identity. One man who showed considerable awareness of this problem was the writer Chingiz Aitmatov who, despite writing mostly in Russian, used his novels to criticise official policies which were depriving Central Asians of their historical memories. Most notable here was *The Day Lasts More Than a Hundred Years* (1980), with its favourable treatment of traditional customs and its reference back to a Mongol practice of binding prisoners' shaven heads with wet camel's skin which when dried squeezed their skulls and was said to destroy their memory. Implicitly Soviet policies were having the same effect in turning the peoples of Central Asia into mankurts (slaves) with no memory of their history or language, and little realisation that they had a heritage which pre-dated 1917.

THE GORBACHEV YEARS AND THE BIRTH OF INDEPENDENT STATEHOOD

The accession of Gorbachev to the leadership of the Soviet Union in 1985 heralded major changes for Central Asia as he sought to re-assert central control. During the brief tenure of Yury Andropov (1982–84) as Soviet leader, a campaign had been launched against the corruption said to permeate regional political life, with special attention paid to the dominance of family connections in party appointments and the failure of many officials to combat seriously traditional customs and ways of life. This assault was restarted and accelerated under Gorbachev who during his first year in office replaced the party leaders of Turkmenistan, Tajikistan and Kyrgyzstan—with those of Uzbekistan and Kazakhstan to follow later—and presided over extensive purges of the administration in all five republics. In early November 1985 it was announced that Kyrgyz party first secretary Turdakun Usubaliev had 'retired' from his position and, though no official explanation was given for this decision, it soon became clear that the archetypal regional boss who had ruled the republic since 1961 had been sacked. This was made plain at a congress of the Kyrgyz Communist Party held in January 1986, where speaker after speaker criticised the style of leadership promoted by their former boss. Addressing the congress the new first secretary Absamat Masaliev criticised the 'violation of Leninist principles of cadres selection' that had taken place, with key officials chosen on the basis of personal loyalty or kinship. This in turn had encouraged a high level of sycophancy which Usubaliev did little to discourage and a style of leadership which was copied at all levels. Other speakers joined in, offering examples of the ways in which those of a more independent nature had been persecuted by the former party leader. Subsequently Usubaliev was expelled from the party, only to be re-admitted the following year.

Despite all this and the removal or reshuffling of around 75% of leading republican and regional officials, Masaliev's tenure of office witnessed little real change. Though purges brought in many younger officials and reduced the size of the party apparatus by 20%, the old guard of central party bureaucrats and regional bosses continued to dominate, and one poll taken in 1988 showed that many party activists had seen few signs of changes in the style of party work.[13] The language of perestroika was increasingly used, and there was some discussion of problem issues such as the declining use of the Kyrgyz language and the economic problems of rural areas, but no energetic policy responses. Indeed many in the republic felt that perestroika's new emphasis on republican self-sufficiency was unfair given the economic structures created by Moscow over the last seven decades. Prime minister Apas Jumagalov, though sympathetic to reform, asked how all the responsibility could be placed on Kyrgyz shoulders when nearly half of Kyrgyzstan's workers were employed by enterprises subordinate to the centre and when capital investment per head was far below the national average. Masaliev, however, remained suspicious of Gorbachev's reform programme and began to develop close links with conservatives in Moscow; people such as Yegor Ligachev who visited the republic in the autumn of 1989. Of particular concern to these traditionalists was the fear that Gorbachev's reforms were likely to undermine rather than strengthen the Soviet system as he claimed. Consequently Masaliev resisted all efforts to create a popular front in Kyrgyzstan and until late 1990 the openness or glasnost developing in other parts of the Soviet Union failed to penetrate this corner of the empire. Conservatism was also evident in Masaliev's speech to the newly elected Soviet Congress of Peoples' Deputies meeting in June 1989 at which he attacked the breakdown in law and order which had allowed extremists to surface, and where he expressed concern as to whether this new fangled Moscow based talking shop had the ability to resolve the country's problems.[14]

This official attitude was not without practical consequences for the republic, as a lethargic leadership failed to tackle mounting social and economic difficulties. The reduction of central involvement had only exacerbated existing problems with an economic downturn leading to a rising tide of unemployment amongst young males in the countryside. From May 1989 a growing number of young people started to congregate in the capital Frunze where they staged a series of demonstrations calling for land to be given to them by the city authorities so that they could build houses. In the summer the settlers formed 'Ashar' (Mutual Help), the first significant independent social organisation to be created in the republic, and under its auspices they began to seize land and build shanty towns on the outskirts of the city. Masaliev agreed to register Ashar, but protests continued into the new year as the authorities demonstrated no genuine desire for dialogue. Simultaneously there began to emerge other social and political organisations a number of whom were to coalesce in the Democratic Movement 'Kyrgyzstan' (DDK) in May 1990. At their founding congress 300 delegates approved a programme calling for market reforms and genuine democratisation, and by the end of the year the movement was claiming a membership of 100,000.

During 1989 this already tense situation was made worse by signs of conflict between the republic's ethnic groups. In September 1989, after considerable debate, the Supreme Soviet had adopted a language law which made Kyrgyz the state language of the republic and described Russian as the language of 'inter-ethnic communication'. One clause of this bill required managerial and administrative personnel to be able to communicate with their subordinates in Kyrgyz, a provision that clearly challenged the current dominance of Slavic elites in most sectors of the economy and administration. Long submerged anti-Russian feeling became apparent as seemingly responsible newspapers published letters attacking the role of Russians in public life, and many Russian speakers began to fear for their future in Kyrgyzstan. In consequence the level of emigration began to rise in early 1990 and continued to do so until 1993, by which time the Russian population had been reduced by 20%. It then slowed down for reasons to be explored in a later chapter.

This situation was made worse by the inter-communal violence that broke out in the Osh region during the summer of 1990. Here local Uzbeks and Kyrgyz came into conflict as a result of tensions engendered by the former's perception that they were unrepresented in local government and the latter's view that the Uzbeks took all the best jobs in the retail and consumer sector. A further grievance was added with the adoption of the state language law which failed to take account of an appeal from Uzbek residents of the southern oblasts of Osh and Jalalabad that some official status be granted Uzbek alongside Russian and Kyrgyz. There had already, in previous years, been a number of conflicts between local Uzbek and Kyrgyz youths, and in the months preceding the violence the local KGB had repeatedly warned the republican authorities that trouble was brewing. In April 1990 Kyrgyz youth activists formed the organisation Osh-aimagy which had sought to acquire more land-holdings for Kyrgyz families, and directed over 500 appeals to this effect to the regional authorities but without success. In consequence they threatened that on 17 June they would start to seize land for themselves. In response the local authorities made a small grant of land from an Uzbek collective farm just outside Osh, a move which ignited Uzbek anger and counter-claims for recognition of Uzbek as a state language and, from some groups, a call for the incorporation of predominantly Uzbek territories into Uzbekistan. As violent clashes spread in the Uzgen district and beyond over 200 were killed before the rioting was contained by the Soviet army and Interior Ministry troops. Events unfolded with biblical overtones as local Kyrgyz, like the Israelites about to flee Egypt, were told to paint their doors red if they were to avoid the destruction of their property, and possibly their lives, by rampaging mobs. In the capital, now renamed Bishkek, demonstrators called for the resignation of the party leadership. According to some accounts, Masaliev was so fearful for his own position that he refused to face the crowds and thus lost what little authority he retained in the public mind.[15]

All of these events served to undermine the image of Kyrgyzstan as a relatively peaceful corner of the USSR and, along with the language law, added to Slavic and European concerns about their future position in the republic. Simultaneously they served to undermine Masaliev's position. Earlier that year he had been chosen as chairman of the newly 'elected' Supreme Soviet,[16] but the events in Osh led to renewed criticism of his conservative leadership. Then, in October 1990, the seemingly pliant parliament refused to elect him to a new executive presidency, charging that he had failed to deal with the economic crisis facing the republic and had mismanaged the events at Osh. Instead they chose a compromise candidate, Askar Akaev, at that time chairman of the republican academy of sciences, a man who had largely made his career outside the Communist Party and spent much of it in Russia. Adopting a very different style than Masaliev the new president spent his second day in office meeting with protestors who had been gathering outside the parliament building, and in subsequent speeches made clear his commitment to furthering the cause of reform.

In pursuit of this end he faced a number of difficulties, stemming in part from his lack of a political base within the republic, and in part from the weakness of the social organisations which supported his reform programme. During 1989–90 a number of political movements had emerged but, with the partial exception of the umbrella organisation of the DDK, none had been able to garner widespread popular support. As elsewhere in the USSR political parties tended to be small affairs, dominated by a few individuals and prone to splits stemming from personal rather than ideological differences. Though Akaev frequently spoke of the need for strong parties if democracy was to develop in Kyrgyzstan, and on occasions sought to sponsor quasi-presidential groups such as National Unity of Kyrgyzstan, they failed to materialise during 1990–91 and were to face many problems in taking root once the republic gained full independence. Nonetheless, under Akaev's guidance Kyrgyzstan became the most pluralistic of the Central Asian states, with a growing range of independent social organisations and a lively press. That this was not purely opportunistic was revealed during the attempted August 1991 coup in Moscow, when Akaev quickly made plain his rejection of the plotters and his support for Boris Yeltsin's struggle with the old order. Resisting pressure from conservative Communists within the republic, the president was able to persuade the military to stay in their barracks, and within a few days of the coup's defeat announced his resignation from the party and the departyisation of state and administrative organs. Though Akaev had supported and continued to support attempts at holding the Soviet union together, at the end of August the Kyrgyz parliament voted for independence from the USSR. Akaev then called for presidential elections in October 1991 and was able to generate considerable support within the republic for his candidacy. Though expressing some embarrassment at the absence of any opposition, Akaev used the campaign to stress his commitment to a revival of Kyrgyz identity but at the same time emphasised his key role in representing the interests of all the peoples of a republic in which the titular nationality made up only 53% of the population. Duly elected by a substantial majority Akaev was to preside over the last days of Kyrgyzstan's existence as a constituent unit of the Soviet Union and to lead it towards a very uncertain status as an independent state.

1   Most of the sources are in Russian with the standard Soviet account of the debate over the ethnic origin of the Kyrgyz being S.M. Abramzon's, *Kirgizy i ikh etnogeneticheskie i istoriko-kul'turnye sviazi* (Leningrad, 1971); for more recent discussions see *Kyrgyzy: Etnogeneticheskie i etnokul'turnye protsessy v drevnosti i srednevekov'e v tsentral'noi azii* (Bishkek, 1996).
2   Much valuable material on the lifestyle of the Kyrgyz and their tribal groupings can be found in the writings of Chokan Valikhanov. See especially, *Sobranie sochinenii v piati tomakh, tom 2* (Alma Ata, 1985), pp. 7–170.
3   See Guy Imart, 'The Islamic impact on traditional Kirgiz ethnicity', in *Nationalities Papers*, 14:1, 1–2, 1986, pp. 65–88.
4   A broad overview of the period discussed in this chapter can be found in T.Koichuev, ed, *Istoriia Kyrgyzov i Kyrgyzstana* (Bishkek, 1996), and on the period up to 1900 in V. Mokrynin & V. Ploskikh, *Istoriia Kyrgyzstana* (Bishkek, 1995).
5   E. Sokol, *The Revolt of 1916 in Central Asia* (Baltimore, 1954); for a more recent account see K. Usenbaev, *1916: Geroicheskie i tragicheskie stranitsy* (Bishkek, 1997).

6   On the national demarcation see S. Sabol, 'The creation of Soviet Central Asia: the 1924 national delimitation', in *Central Asian Survey*, 14: 2, 1995, pp. 225–42.

7   Chingiz Aitmatov, *Tales of the Mountains and Steppes*, (Moscow, Progress Publishers, 1977), pp. 236–9.

8   Ibid., p. 16.

9   In 1997 the Kyrgyz State Museum had an exhibition on the position of women in Kyrgyzstan, which included many interesting photographs from the khudzhum period.

10 A Kyrgyz scholar's overview of religious life in Central Asia is offered in A. Tabyshalieva, *Vera v Turkestane* (Bishkek, 1993).

11 Kyrgyz scholars are currently investigating the archives of the state and security police for this period, and about 10,000 people have been formally rehabiliated. Brief accounts can be found in Koichuev, *Istoriia Kyrgyzov i Kyrgyzstana*, pp. 210–22, and T. Koichuev, V. Mokrynin & V. Ploskhikh, *Kyrgyzy i ikh predki* (Bishkek, 1994), pp. 74–7.

12 The text of this can be found in *KPSS v rezoliutsiiakh i resheniiakh s'ezdov, konferentsii i plenumov TsK, Tom. 9* (Moscow, 1983), pp. 264–70.

13 T. Koichueva, ed, *Deistvennost' faktorov perestroikoi* (Frunze, 1990), p. 209.

14 Extracts from some of these speeches can be found in O. Glebov & J. Crowfoot, eds, *The Soviet Empire—Its Nations Speak Out* (New York, 1989), pp. 137–57.

15 T. Razakov, *Oshskie sobytiia—na materialakh KGB* (Bishkek, 1993).

16 On these elections see E. Huskey, 'The rise of contested politics in Central Asia: elections in Kyrgyzstan, 1989–90', in *Europe-Asia Studies*, 47: 5, 1995, pp. 809–29.

Chapter 2

ISLAND OF DEMOCRACY?
THE POLITICS OF INDEPENDENCE

Having acquired independence Kyrgyzstan very quickly gained a reputation as an 'island of democracy' located in a sea of dictatorships and countries ravaged by civil strife. This chapter explores the politics of transition, starting with the constitutional changes introduced in 1992–93, and then examining the rise of 'civil society', the role of informal politics, the attempts to preserve ethnic harmony and encourage an inclusive sense of citizenship. I then go on to analyse the gradual restriction of political space that became apparent from mid-1994, characterised by attacks on the media, the manipulation of election results—not always to the advantage of the president—and the extension of presidential power pushed through at the beginning of 1996. Though it would be difficult to describe this tiny mountainous country as a liberal democracy, it should not be forgotten that in the relatively inhospitable context of Central Asia, Kyrgyzstan retains a considerable degree of social pluralism and a more open political space than any of its Central Asian neighbours.

BUILDING A NEW POLITICAL ORDER, 1991–94

Following the collapse of the Soviet Union many of the successor states, lacking any experience of self government let alone democratic politics, have found the shape of their new politics very much determined by the character and style of the leader in power at the time independence was gained. In the case of Kyrgyzstan, this person was Askar Akaev. Born into a family of collective farm workers in the Kemin district of the Chu valley, Akaev early on showed academic promise and went off to study in Leningrad. It was here that he made his early career, pursuing post-graduate studies in optical physics and eventually gaining a doctorate. In 1976 he returned to work in Frunze, but did not join the Communist Party until 1981 and even then he appears to have preferred to concentrate on his scholarly activities. This relative peace was brought to an end in 1986 when he was drafted into the Kyrgyz party's department of science and education, though one year later he left this position on being selected as deputy chairman of the republic's academy of sciences, and in 1989 he was appointed to head this prestigous body.

It was this seemingly non-political scientist who parliamentary deputies selected as president of Kyrgyzstan in October 1990, as a potentially controllable compromise candidate. Akaev, however, appears to have had other ideas, and quickly made clear his commitment to reform. In his first address to the assembled deputies, he stressed the achievements of his country which stemmed in part from the new energies released by Gorbachev's perestroika, but pointed to the many problems still facing it. In such circumstances a market based economy was urgently needed, and this was a task that would demand 'the mobilisation of all the creative forces and energy of society, and the intellectual potential of leaders at all levels'. At the same time he emphasised that the market was no panacea, warning that it could not replace hard and creative work by officials and the population.[1] In a programmatic speech delivered in December 1991 Akaev argued that the only way forward was through 'the development of private interest, private life, and private property' based upon a strong civil society, guarantees of civil and political rights, ethnic harmony, and social protection for those likely to find the transition period difficult. Simultaneously he claimed that the reality of the situation, and the complexity of the tasks faced, required that there be strong executive power capable of pushing through reform against the resistance of vested interests. Even then it would require good luck and skilful leadership if stabilisation of the economy was to be achieved in the next three to four years.[2]

In subsequent speeches Akaev made frequent references to the need for marketisation and democratisation to move forward together and, following his selection as president, he showed his openness to newly emerging social forces by meeting with representatives of various groups that had been picketing the parliamentary gathering and then holding a series of meetings with leaders of informal social organisations. At these meetings the new president repeatedly emphasised that whilst he was committed to building a sovereign Kyrgyzstan, this was to be a republic in which civil and ethnic harmony was to take priority, and he warned that he would not tolerate the promotion of ethnic exclusivity. And meeting with the leaders of national cultural centres and social organisations in February 1992 he reminded them that the goal of democratisation demanded that priority be given to the rights of the individual rather than those of the nation, and emphasised the need for special sensitivity to the concerns of the substantial Russian minority.[3]

In seeking to build this new, democratic political order Akaev had to work with a constitution created and a parliament elected under the old Soviet order. Parliamentary elections in February 1990 had returned 350 deputies to the Supreme Soviet, though the electoral contest was far less open than in most of the western regions of the USSR and the electoral process was flawed in a number of ways. For example, the granting of nomination rights to labour collectives, educational establishments and military units gave a considerable advantage to the party apparatus, a trend reinforced by the activities of the central electoral commission which had the final say in the registration of candidates. On the day a 92% turnout was reported, with much higher levels of participation in the south and the countryside where local bosses could exercise greater control over the population. Moreover, despite competition for many seats, most of the party bosses chose to run in areas where there were no alternative candidates. In consequence party officials, enterprise directors, collective and state farm chairmen, and officials took the majority of seats, though a few critical voices were to be found in the new parliament, notably Topchubek Turgunaliev, then a minor party functionary, who was to be a leading oppositionist during the 1990s.[4]

This body very much represented the Kyrgyz elite. Most came from privileged positions, from the families that had dominated the political system during the Soviet period; most were committed to the existing political order, albeit, in some cases, to a reformed version. Though some quickly took on board nationalist demands, many within the parliamentary and administrative elite had only a tenuous connection to their national culture, having been brought up within Russian educational establishments and spent most of their lives working within Soviet institutions. Typical of such people was Feliks Kulov, who became Akaev's vice-president, despite his inability to speak his native Kyrgyz with any degree of fluency.

Though many of these deputies opted for Akaev in October 1990, this did not represent a clear body of support for the marketisation and democratisation that he increasingly advocated, with many parliamentarians fearful that such reforms would threaten their economic well being and political influence. Some of these differences were to come to a head in debates over the passing of a new constitution in 1992–3 and were to lead Akaev in 1994 to push through a 'self-dissolution' of parliament. Various draft constitutions started to circulate in the spring of 1992 but persistent differences led to the postponement of debate until the autumn when a new draft text was subject to criticism from Akaev for placing virtually all power in parliamentary hands and ignoring the realities of a situation where strong executive power was necessary to hold the country together and push through reform. Then from late 1992 until April 1993 the constitution was subject to an extensive public discussion in the media and in parliament.

A wide range of issues were discussed during this debate: the question of economic rights, the status of the Russian language, the position of women, and the question of whether the constitution should make some reference to the values promoted by the state.[5] Early on in the discussion Akaev suggested that the preamble should make some reference to the importance of the moral values of Islam and other religions, whilst others wanted more prescriptive moral injunctions such as the duty of all citizens to respect older people. More controversial, however, were debates over the issue of political power and in particular the relationship between president and parliament. Speaking at a meeting with party leaders in February 1993, Akaev warned of the dangers of a Russian style confrontation between president and parliament and, though tensions were never as great as in Moscow, each body sought to enhance its powers within the new constitution. A number of those writing to the papers expressed concern that many of the articles of the constitution were too vaguely phrased, thus leaving room for conflict in the future. In particular there were comments about the ambiguities of the president's position in the original draft where he was described as head of state, though the same text vested executive power in a prime minister whose political relations with the president were unclearly defined. A number of contributors to the debate wanted to see a president with strong powers, but the communist party expressed concern that though Akaev himself could be trusted with such powers, a powerful executive presidency could be abused by a less scrupulous individual. Others expressed concern over so much political power being vested in central institutions. One called for an extension of 'people's power' by reducing the number of signatures required for a referendum from 300,000 to 100,000, and those for the right of legislative initiative from 30,000 to 5,000. Others wanted greater powers to be given to local soviets with the current system, whereby the president appointed administrators to head each of the country's six regions, being replaced by an elective system in which those chosen were responsible to the soviet and its electors.

In practice the final draft put before parliament was relatively balanced in its distribution of powers when compared to that of most neighbouring states. Addressing parliament, Akaev reported on the evolution of the discussion, noting the dropping of references to the moral values of Islam, the rejection of the definition of Russian as the language of inter-ethnic communication though guarantees for minority languages had been strengthened, and pointed to the clearly separate roles of parliament and president. Under the final document. approved by parliament on 5 May, Kyrgyzstan was described as 'a sovereign, unitary, democratic republic built upon the basis of a legal, secular state' and 'the carriers of sovereignty were the people of Kyrgyzstan' (Article 1). In terms of political structures provision was made for the future election of a smaller, 105 seat professional assembly called the Zhogorku Kenesh (Supreme Council or Soviet)—a use of the Kyrgyz title which was rather tenuously seen as a reversion to the tribal assemblies of earlier days. This body had the power to approve key presidential appointments, to legislate, and to over-ride presidential vetoes of legislation in certain circumstances. The president—who had to be a citizen of Kyrgyzstan, over 35 years old, know the state language and have been resident in the republic for at least 15 years—was given the power to appoint the prime minister and other key officials with the approval of parliament, to initiate legislation and to dissolve parliament before the end of its term providing this was approved in a referendum. Though the president was described as exercising control over the government and had the right to attend its meetings, the prime minister was given full responsibility for the day to day running of its affairs. The new constitution also guaranteed citizens a wide range of civil and political rights so long as these were exercised within the framework of the law.[6]

Interviewed after the adoption of the constitution, Akaev described it as a major step forward in the democratic development of Kyrgyzstan and rejected the view that the republic was not ready for democracy. To support this contention he pointed to the election of khans and processes of consultation within clan structures during pre-Soviet times, though he accepted that the democratic ethic was far from fully developed amongst the Kyrgyz. Subsequent events, however, were to make him more wary of the influence of the clan structure and more susceptible to the opinion that in fact Central Asia was indeed not really prepared for the advent of pluralistic politics which, if taken too far too quickly, might endanger the security and stability of fragile new states.

Despite the adoption of the constitution tensions between the parliament and the executive remained, with constant sniping directed at the government of prime minister Tursunbek Chyngyshev and, implicitly, at Akaev. Two issues dominated: the ongoing economic decline which left much of the population in poverty, and allegations of corruption, especially surrounding the awarding of contracts to foreign investors and the development of the Kumtor gold field. In mid-December 1993 a parliamentary vote of no-confidence in the government, though lacking the necessary two-thirds majority, led Akaev to dismiss the government and in January to appoint Apas Jumagalov—the last Soviet era prime minister—as head of a new administration. Other personnel changes followed, with Communist Party leader Jumgalbek Amanbaev coopted as a deputy prime-minister and Feliks Kulov, the former vice-president rendered redundant by the omission of that post in the new constitutional order, appointed as governor (akim) of the northern Chu region. Yet the reshuffling of leaders did little to ease the sense of political crisis, with parliamentary life characterised by persistent squabbling and deputies often seeming more concerned to profit from their positions than to pass laws. Typical of these difficulties was the failure to adopt a new law on the election of deputies because of disagreements over such issues as whether parliamentarians could simultaneously hold official positions. Parliamentary speaker Medetkhan Sherimkulov, a strong critic of Akaev and the government's handling of the award of contracts for the development of the republic's gold industry, but also a man committed to preserving political peace, sought to bring the deputies into line but faced an uphill battle. For his part, Akaev decided to bolster his own legitimacy through a referendum held at the end of January 1994 which asked the people whether they supported the policies of the president and wanted him to remain in office until the scheduled end of term in October 1996. Predictably some 96% of the population turned out to vote and 95% said yes, a result the president took as representing a mandate to continue with current policies. In subsequent weeks Akaev, together with prime minister Apas Jumugalov, gave a series of speeches calling for parliament to act more speedily to pass laws supportive of the economic reform process.

When such admonitions appeared to fail Akaev supported, or engineered, a campaign for the early self-dissolution of parliament, taking advantage of divisions within that body. During July 1994, 105 of the 323 deputies, many of them ministers or regional and local leaders appointed to their positions by the president, signed a letter accusing parliamentary leaders of sabotaging reform and called for a referendum on the creation of a new two chamber parliament. Simultaneously a number of parties issued a call for joint parliamentary and presidential elections. In response, speaker Sherimkulov pointed out that deputies had previously ignored his call for fresh elections, and rejected charges that he was using parliament as a basis for opposition to the president. He also pointed out that during constitutional debates a two chamber assembly had been seen as unnecessary unless a federal state was proposed.[7] In practice the motives of many of those involved in calling for new elections were somewhat ambiguous as they saw in dissolution a way of preventing the completion of a major parliamentary investigation of corruption amongst deputies, which also might have exposed the dubious activities of some officials close to Akaev. By September 168 deputies had joined the boycott of parliament and in effect made it unworkable. In response the government resigned on the grounds that it could not function without a parliament, after which Akaev dissolved parliament and proposed a referendum to be held on 22 October. Here the electors were to be asked to affirm that future constitutional changes would be made by referendum rather than parliament and approve the creation of a new, two-chamber professional parliament. Once this was affirmed by 72.1% of the population, a constitutional convention was called to discuss further changes and elections were scheduled for the end of the year, though these were later postponed until February 1995.

DEVELOPING AN OPEN SOCIETY

From the outset Askar Akaev made frequent reference to the need to create a civil society which would underpin both democratisation and marketisation. In particular he stressed the importance of the development of a broad range of social organisations and an open but constructive media operating within the confines of the rule of law. What was less clear was how the president and political elite saw this essentially Western construct developing in a society where the primary ties were rooted in collective links to kin and region, rather than based upon common participation as individuals in social organisations. Nonetheless the notion of civil society rapidly became de rigeur for aspiring political leaders; in Akaev's case perhaps combining an initial rather naive belief that many of the conditions found in Western industrialised democracies could be replicated in Central Asia with a realisation that the use of such language and the development of a law based state would be useful to attract foreign investors. Whereas his predecessor Absamat Masaliev had proved resistant to the free development of 'civil society', Askar Akaev encouraged it and by 1992 Kyrgyzstan was probably the most open of the Central Asian polities, with a lively media, and an ever growing number of social organisations and political movements.

Most academic accounts of civil society stress the importance of a relatively free information space within which social groups and movements can exchange views, offer a critique of others and inform the public about their activities. Following Akaev's election in October 1990, the official media began to develop a more independent stance, and soon there emerged a number of quasi-autonomous papers each with their own editorial line and often adopting a highly critical position towards the political establishment. Typical of the government papers was *Sovetskaya kirgiziya*, renamed *Slovo kyrgyzstana* at the end of February 1992. Dropping its stodgy reporting of party gatherings and economic statistics of doubtful significance, the paper began to explore the political issues of the day in a more informative way, reporting the activities and programmes of embryonic political parties, profiling key politicians, publishing critical articles and letters from the public. Others papers followed, though offering varying styles and differing levels of political involvement. Amongst the more critical were to be the parliamentary paper *Svobodny gory* (Free Mountains) which increasingly subjected the presidential team to attack, and the weekly *Res publika*, established in early 1992, which waged war on corruption and what it saw as the growing authoritarianism encouraged by the presidential apparat—though on occasion it had a tendency to follow the lead of Britain's *Private Eye* in publishing semi-libellous stories for which it lacked sufficient evidence.

Less critical were television and radio, for though several private radio and television stations were to emerge in the early 1990s—at least one of which was far more interested in showing pornography than entering the political arena—most of the population watched or listened to the state controlled stations which remained supportive of the government or to Russian stations which largely ignored Kyrgyz affairs.

All media outlets continued to face problems with distribution and finance, the latter stemming in large part from the reduction of government subsidies and the inability of an impoverished population to purchase papers. These were particularly acute outside the capital where the old elites controlled much of the media and where more critical outlets were often closed down by regional bosses who controlled the finances. Early on there were signs that Akaev was becoming impatient with some newspapers, seeing them as offering largely destructive criticism at a time when the country had to pull together to climb out of the crisis situation. Addressing a meeting of editors in June 1992 the president stressed that democracy equalled freedom plus responsibility and singled out *Res publika* for what he saw as its persistent efforts to discredit the authorities. The paper's correspondents were subsequently to be excluded from the press briefings of the presidential apparat. In October and November 1993 the government and procuracy issued various decrees which appeared to curtail freedom and restore some degree of censorship and, though these were quickly disowned by officials, many journalists feared that they marked the beginning of new restraints on press freedom. For all this Kyrgyzstan's media retained a degree of independence that would be the envy of most Central Asian journalists and not until mid-1994 were the fears of critical journalists to be realised when the parliamentary paper *Svobodny gory* was, at the suggestion of Akaev, closed down by the courts.

The first half of the decade also witnessed an explosion in the number of social organisations and political movements or parties. In February 1991 Akaev signed the law on social organisations which created a framework for the activities of associations, interest groups and political parties. Defined as 'voluntarily formed, created as a result of the free choice of citizens of the Republic of Kyrgyzstan on the basis of common interests, aims and principles', social organisations were required to register with the Ministry of Justice if they were to acquire the status of persons in law. Only those bodies which promoted ethnic or religious hatred, or which posed a threat to the sovereignty of the republic were to be banned, and the law carefully set out the conditions under which registration could be refused and offered an appeals procedure for those denied a legal existence. Finally, in the event that the law clashed with any international agreements adhered to by Kyrgyzstan it was stated that the latter would prevail.[8]

In practice the law was interpreted in a relatively liberal fashion during the early 1990s and there emerged a wide variety of legally recognised organisations. By February 1993 the Justice Ministry had registered 258 social organisations—a number that would reach nearly 1000 by the summer of 1997—including 15 political movements or parties, 31 professional bodies, 21 national-cultural centres or organisations, 41 sporting bodies, 11 children's and young people's and 5 women's organisations. During the law's first two years in operation only four organisations were refused registration—the Islamic Centre, the Uighur Freedom Organisation, the Social Democrats of Kyrgyzstan and the Semirech'e Cossacks, whilst the Communist Party which lost its registration in the aftermath of the coup was later to regain it in early 1992. At the same time there functioned an array of social organisations, often of an ephemeral nature, which did not seek official authorisation, and which, though lacking the status of a juridical person, were not deemed illegal.[9]

Leaving aside political parties, many of the grandly titled committees, organisations and federations were the offspring of enthusiastic entrepreneurs promoting their own hobby horses or created in order to garner grants and foreign trips from bodies such as the Soros Foundation, the Danielle Mitterand Fund or the European Union. Some focused on particular issues such as human rights or the environment, whilst others were created to defend the sectoral interests of particular social groups, including the homeless, women or workers. Of the latter trade unions and peasant groups have been especially active since 1992, offering sharp critiques of government policies which have left much of the population in poverty. During the constitutional debates of 1992–93 the independent trade unions frequently called for an explicit textual defence of the right to work and more recently have reacted sharply to the persistent delays that many workers and pensioners experience in being paid or receiving their pensions. Nonetheless, many workers have claimed that the activism of the trade unions, evident in the issuing of proclamations and complaints, has not been matched by much involvement in the workplace.

From the last years of perestroika single issue groups were important in the development of Kyrgyz civil society, with early political crises stimulated by the actions of homeless squatters around the capital and the subsequent creation of Ashar (Mutual Help) to agitate for their needs. Such activities were taken up by various social defence groups created during the early 1990s, who argued for measures such as the indexation of pensions and social policies geared to social protection rather than private profit. In mid-1997 the actions of the Yntymak (Agreement) movement, which brought hundreds of homeless and unemployed young men to the capital, mostly from the Naryn region, created considerable controversy as the authorities and Bishkek citizens proved divided as how best to resolve their problems.[10] Whilst such groups have impinged upon the political process, and in many respects have raised more important long term questions for the authorities, other issue groups have come more directly into conflict with the authorities. Notable amongst these were the various human rights groups which, as we shall see below, found themselves increasingly at odds with the government from 1995 onwards.

Nonetheless, during the early 1990s an embryonic, modern civil society was gradually emerging within Kyrgyzstan, or at least within the capital. By and large social organisations were tolerated by the state, though officials became wary of those with close connections to opposition politicians. It was also the case that many of the new social organisations carried out their work away from the limelight, especially those concerned with welfare, the environment, women's rights, agricultural support and self-help projects. Perhaps inevitably, the birth of civil society in the Western or narrow political scientist's sense was beset by problems. Many of the organisations so proudly announced—the vast majority of which were to be found in Bishkek—ceased to function almost immediately, with some sources estimating that as few as 20% of social organisations actually functioned in a meaningful way. Moreover, there was considerable duplication, evident in the the multiplicity of women's groups that emerged, each claiming to tackle very similar issues such as violence against women, reproductive rights, welfare provision, the upbringing of children and so forth.[11] And, as already suggested, in the context of a society that had little experience of open politics and where kinship ties remained powerful, it was to be expected that progress would be slow and that civil society's form might be different from that assumed by outside observers.[12]

Another sphere where Kyrgyzstan offered greater freedom than most of its neighbours lay in the area of religious liberty. Though Akaev had frequently stressed the need to protect society from the threat of religious extremism, during the early 1990s this posed little real danger to Kyrgyzstan's security except insofar as the conflict in Tajikistan might have spilt over the borders. Within the country there was no sign of a religiously based political movement acquiring substantial support, in large part because of the religious heritage of the region. Though nominally Muslim, the Kyrgyz nomads, especially in the northern regions, have traditionally been extremely undogmatic in their religious beliefs, and through much of the country a largely syncretic Islam has emerged blending age old customs with more orthodox Muslim teachings. Notable here has been the reverence given to extravagant mazars or tombs of Muslim 'saints' which have been places of pilgrimage for those seeking health care and fertility, a trend which some suggest has increased in the post-Soviet era with the decay of official welfare provision. This limited Islamicisation was further reinforced during the Soviet era when the vast majority of mosques were closed and the possibility of legally teaching religion to children ended. In the northern regions Islamic rites may have acompanied rites of passage but few had a very sound knowledge of Islamic teaching. During a visit to a Naryn region farm settlement in August 1997, I was told of a recent funeral where the Islamic establishment had been represented by a small boy who could only mutter a few verses of the Koran in Arabic. The position was different in the southern regions, especially in the Fergana valley. Here religion retained a much more important role and, though mosques and religious institutions have opened across the republic in recent years, it is in the two southern regions, with an estimated 1,000 plus mosques, that the revitalisation of Islam has been most evident.

At the same time, Kyrgyzstan became a regional haven for a wide variety of religious movements, benefitting from the government's relatively laissez faire approach to religion.[13] In consequence, numerous American, European, and South Korean missionary groups have been active, whilst Bishkek has become a centre for Jehovah's Witnesses, Bahais and other groups often denied access to other republics in the region. Unlike some of the former Soviet states which sought to ban proselytisation, or effectively favour certain religious groups, the Kyrgyz government preferred to keep out of religious matters. In 1992, when some Islamic activists sought a ban on foreign missionaries, Akaev remained neutral on the ground that there was little protection for ethnic Kyrgyz or Uzbeks who converted to Christianity and social pressures often resulted in ostracism and beatings for converts.[14] Yet, as we shall see, this attitude became increasingly hard to maintain as numerous religious groups began to operate in Kyrgyzstan and there arose growing pressures from both the state and more traditional groups for greater controls over the activities of 'cults and sects'.

One further area where there was some attempt to emulate Western models lay in the creation of political parties. From the very beginning, President Akaev spoke of his desire to see the emergence of a coherent and strong multi-party democracy, and during his first two or three years in power held frequent meetings with the leaders of political parties. Yet little effort was made to facilitate the emergence of strong parties. Akaev initially acted in ways that sought to coopt parties into the ruling coalition, but then became increasingly critical of the failure of parties to develop, claiming that such groups as had been created were beset by a negativism that was quick to criticise the government but had little positive to offer. Moreover, as happened in other former Soviet states, there was a tendency for the parties that did spring up to be dominated by powerful and ambitious personalities, often with links to particular regions, who failed to develop mass organisations capable of mobilising substantial sections of the population.

Of the parties that did emerge, the Communists were to prove the strongest in organisational terms, able to build on a tradition and membership from before 1991 and possessing an experienced leadership which quickly overcame the disadvantage of having supported the August coup. Formally refounded in June 1992, the party became an increasingly vocal critic of economic reform which it saw as leading the country to bankruptcy and resulting in the unnecessary sale of national assets to appease foreign economic interests. In March 1993 Jumgalbek Amanbaev was elected leader of the party, but after he was coopted as a deputy prime minister by Akaev at the beginning of 1994, the party elected S. Sydykov as leader and then in late summer 1995 returned former first secretary Absamat Masaliev to the helm. From this base he launched his candidature for the presidency in December 1995 and in the event proved the main challenger to Akaev in the latter's bid for re-election.

The Communists also had the greatest numerical strength, claiming some 25,000 members and active party organisations through most of the country. Yet their numbers disguised considerable weakness stemming from an ageing membership often out of touch with the aspirations of younger, more nationalistically inclined Kyrgyz. And in this they shared much in common with groups such as the Agrarian Labour Party and the Movement for Brotherhood and Union which, not without some justification, saw many of Kyrgyzstan's problems as stemming from the precipitate collapse of the USSR but, rather naively and nostalgically, saw salvation largely in terms of a recreation of the wider integrated union.

Many of the other parties that emerged in the early 1990s had their roots in the broad based Democratic Movement of Kyrgyzstan (DDK) created in

May 1990. An umbrella movement encompassing a variety of social and political groups, the DDK spent the last 18 months of the USSR's existence arguing the case for extending and making a reality of Kyrgyzstan's independence. Though claiming a commitment to the preservation of ethnic harmony, the vast majority of those involved were ethnic Kyrgyz, a fact that alienated potential Slavic democrats and liberals. Moreover its critics claimed that it was an organisation incapable of constructive action, good at mobilising crowds at times of crisis, as during the events in Osh during 1990 or those of August 1991, but otherwise able only to offer the slogans of democracy, civil society and economic reform rather than any real policy content. By mid-1991 splits were emerging within the movement, as some sought to radicalise the DDK and turn it into a political party. In June 1993 a DDK party was indeed created and later registered by the Justice Ministry with a claimed membership of 700.

By the time the DDK set about creating its own party organisation the wider movement had been subject to a number of splits as more radical nationalists sought to increase the pace of reform. At the time one of the more significant of these appeared likely to be Erkin Kyrgyzstan (ErK), created by Topchubek Turgunaliev, Omurbek Tekebaev and others in February 1991. Describing itself as a democratic party committed to the creation of a law governed state, ErK adopted a more nationalistic position and a critical attitude towards the government which quickly alienated even some of its own leaders and further splits followed. In late 1992 Omurbek Tekebaev and several other founding members broke away and formed the Ata Meken (Fatherland) Party which described itself as centrist and as willing to offer constructive criticism to the government. In subsequent years ErK was subject to further divisions as two prima donnas—Turgunaliev and Tursunbai Bakir uulu—came into conflict, the former adopted an uncompromising critique of Akaev's reforms which led to his imprisonment in early 1997. The latter, claiming to represent the true spirit of ErK, was elected to parliament in February 1995 where he initially sustained a sharp critique of the government in both the chamber and the opposition press, before experiencing a Damascus road like conversion in mid-1996 which turned him into a qualified supporter of the government and scourge of the opposition.[15]

The most radical nationalist positions were expressed by Asaba whose chairman, when asked his views on the rights of other nationalities in June 1992, was to reply that his party's chief aim was to defend the rights and interests of the Kyrgyz people and that therefore it had no interest in other nationalities. Since then Asaba has taken a consistently nationalist line, attacking Akaev when he sought to modify the status of the Russian language and following hints that Kyrgyzstan might be willing to allow dual citizenship to ethnic Russians. At the same time Asaba has engaged in a series of disputes with Cossack organisations which led one of them in early 1997 to call for the removal of the party's registration for stirring up ethnic hatred against the Russian population.

Other parties which sprang up in the early 1990s adopted essentially centrist positions, critical of the government on certain issues but essentially loyal to Akaev and his reform programme. Typical of these was the Republican Peoples Party which claimed to represent all nationalities and expressed commitment to a social democratic position. Criticising what it described as the posture politics of Communists and nationalists alike, it saw no alternative to Akaev but called for greater government attention to the social defence of the population. Another party that adopted a moderately critical position was the Democratic Party of Women created in time for the February 1995 parliamentary elections whose leader Tokon Shalieva was subsequently elected to parliament. For this party one of the key issues was the impact of economic reform and the revitalisation of patriarchal customs for the women of Kyrgyzstan who had traditionally enjoyed considerable freedom within society. In the run up to the second round of voting in 1995, in which only 7 of the 82 candidates were women, Shalieva suggested that a parliament without women would be like a family without any roots, and called on men and women alike to ensure that there were at least some female deputies.[16]

Though many of these parties appeared limited in their appeal and basis, the early 1990s witnessed some attempts to create broader coalition movements or 'catch-all' parties. In March 1993 a Congress of Democratic Forces, with Akaev and prime minister Chyngyshev in attendance, was convened to bring together various political forces, but the attempt to create a broad movement failed after more radical elements led by Asaba and ErK called for the resignation of the government. In subsequent months further gatherings were held but most suffered the same fate as the ambitions and objectives of individual leaders clashed and as the radical democrats adopted an increasingly critical stance towards Akaev and the government. There were also various attempts to set up quasi-presidential parties, groups such as Peoples Unity created in July 1991 and the Party of Unity of Kyrgyzstan (PEK) created in April 1994 and initially chaired by the head of the State Economic Committee Amangeldy Muraliev. More successful than either of these was to be the Social Democratic Party of Kyrgyzstan (SDPK) not to be confused with an earlier creation, the Association of Social Democrats. The founding congress of this body was held in July 1993 and adopted a fairly general programme committing the party to the defence of Kyrgyz sovereignty, different forms of property, close ties with the former Soviet states, and social defence of the population. In a later discussion document they expressed their concern at the migration of Russian speakers, suggested the reinstatement of Russian as the language of inter-ethnic communication in the constitution and a greater degree of ethnic proportionality in the selection of cadres. At first the SDPK looked like another well intentioned attempt to create a broad coalition that would founder in the same way as others, but during the parliamentary elections of February 1995 the party was the most successful of all the parties, gaining 14 of the 105 seats. Only around 30 deputies had any formal party affiliation. By 1996 many were speaking of the SDPK as the party of power, pointing to a membership dominated by regional administrators, leading businessmen, and representatives of the political establishment. Yet in practice the party has failed to develop a meaningful organisation throughout the country and remains a party of notables.

Despite the proliferation, there was little evidence to suggest that the population was developing any clear sense of party identification. A series of polls carried out in 1994 found that few parties enjoyed substantial levels of support amongst the population, that nearly 20% of those surveyed had no intention of voting in forthcoming elections and up to 50% said that they would have difficulty in choosing a party. In the first poll carried out in February only the Communists with 21.6% were backed by a significant percentage of the population. By September their total had fallen to 9.45% closely followed by the moderate nationalist Ata Meken party with 8.65%. But more striking in the latter poll was the declining level of party identification with 67.5% attaching themselves to no party label. Moreover, these national figures disguised considerable regional and demographic variations. For example, in the Naryn oblast some 60% linked themselves to a specific party; in the capital Bishkek, where most political activists were based, the figure was below 20%; and in the Talas region over 83% said they would not vote or found it hard to answer about which party they would support (see Table 1). Others figures showed that Russians were more likely to vote for the Communists and that young people were less likely to do so, and in June 1994 ErK was the party most likely to be supported by the highly educated (at 12.97%). The limited nature of popular support for political parties was further born out when elections were held in February 1995 and only about a third of the seats went to candidates standing under party labels.

Table 1:   At future elections for which political party would you vote?

	Total	Bishkek	Chui obl	Issyk Kul obl	Talas obl	Naryn obl	Osh obl	Jalalabad obl
Number polled	2000	276	338	190	90	120	622	364
Communists	9.45	7.61	2.37	9.47	10	27.5	10.93	8.79
Ata Meken	8.65	2.17	2.37	0.53	0	12.5	15.43	12.91
ErK	4.5	2.54	5.33	2.63	2.22	3.33	6.75	3.3
DDK	3.6	2.9	2.66	4.21	0	8.33	4.98	1.65
Asaba	2.2	1.45	0.89	1.58	1.11	0.83	4.87	0.55
SDPK	1.15	1.45	0.89	0	0	1.67	1.77	0.82
Agrarians	1.10	0	1.78	1.05	1.11	2.5	1.13	0.82
RPP	0.85	0.72	0.59	0	0	1.67	0.64	1.92
Will not take part	19.05	30.8	31.66	17.89	5.56	4.17	14.63	14.84
Difficult to answer	48.45	50	51.46	61.59	77.78	35.00	37.63	53.50

Source: *Slovo Kyrgyzstana* 24 September 1994

The failure of political parties to emerge as major political forces stems from a number of factors, including the ambiguity of official attitudes. Many officials have remained suspicious of alternative power centres and the president's support has not extended beyond rhetoric. Indeed it might be argued that the institutional choices made by the political elites have created disincentives for party development. Where parliament is not central there are fewer compulsions on deputies to act within the framework of organised and disciplined groupings, and more to be gained by the evolution of shifting coalitions of interest which deputies use to promote their own ideological visions or to pursue private or regional goals. At the same time parties themselves are not without responsibility. All too often they have been based upon personalities and regions, and have paid insufficient attention to the creation of nationwide organisations with broad agendas, despite the adoption of single member constituencies and a majority electoral system which might be thought to encourage the creation of such parties. Perhaps more importantly, the evolution of national political parties has probably been undermined by the continued importance of regional patronage networks and tribalism which we discuss below.

The weakness of parties has led to some public discussion of how their effectiveness might be improved. Whilst Akaev has adopted an increasingly negative tone, attacking radical democrats for unthinking efforts to impose abstract Western models on Kyrgyzstan and criticising the inability of parties to cooperate, others have sought practical solutions. The chairman of the Party of Unity of Kyrgyzstan suggested a ballot after which the two leading parties would be given state support, whilst deputy Tursunbai Bakir uulu has called for a mixed proportional system with a 3% barrier that has to be jumped for representation in parliament. More recently Akaev has come out in favour of a quota based electoral system in which parties, women and national minorities are given some form of guaranteed representation in the assembly. Whether such devices would be able to overcome traditional and informal control of politics rooted in the regions is far from clear.

THE IMPORTANCE OF INFORMAL POLITICS

One of the key problems facing the development of a civil society, and the evolution of a 'modern' polity throughout Central Asia, has been the continued strength of informal politics rooted in what some have described as 'tribalism', a word generally given negative connotations. Prior to Soviet rule most people identified themselves with extended family groups, tribes and regions, and had little sense of belonging to a wider ethnic group. During the seventy years of Communist rule, some effort was made by the centre to undermine these local identities by encouraging closer identification with the nation, albeit one that was heavily Sovietised and dependent upon the Russian 'elder brother'. In consequence the importance of kinship groups may have been attenuated somewhat, especially for those Kyrgyz who settled in the major cities. At the same time, Communist rule reinforced as well as changed such linkages, for when the centre took all the key policy decisions the use of local networks often proved the only means of national self-defence, enabling patrons and their clients to circumvent the more onerous demands of the system. Particularly in the rural regions local political life tended to revolve around patronage networks rooted in kinship and regionally based groups, though over time these have been partially extended beyond a narrow sense of related people with shared genealogies to include members of other clans and ethnic groups who have been effectively coopted into existing political families. These in turn have had ramifications at the centre leading Akaev to suggest in November 1992 that in partially democratic Kyrgyzstan, clans remained far more powerful political actors than any of the new parties then springing up. Yet whilst the importance of such informal political connections is often stressed, it remains hard for the outsider to analyse the precise role and workings of 'tribalism'.

Historically one of the key divisions has been between the northern and southern Kyrgyz, which on occasions has appeared to threaten efforts at holding the republic together. With the northerner Askar Akaev replacing the southerner Absamat Masaliev there were claims that appointments were increasingly dominated by the north, with special prominence given to those from the Talas and Chu regions. This in turn was reinforced by the economics of independence. The north has proved quicker to adapt to market oriented refom than the south where anti-market attitudes have reinforced political suspicions about northern dominance.[17] Such attitudes are reinforced by a cultural superiority complex on the part of some northerners, evident in the reluctance of Bishkek officials or northern army officers to serve in Osh or Jalalabad regions and the dismissive comments one sometimes hears about the primitive nature of southern culture which allows 'fundamentalism' to spread. During much of the 1990s, opposition to Akaev's rule has come from the south, with the networks associated with Bekmamat Osmanov (d. 1997) and others playing a key role. In October 1992 Akaev flew to Jalalabad region to oversee the removal of this controversial figure as head of the regional adminstration. Osmanov had reinforced his position by appointing his seven brothers to key posts, but was forced to offer his resignation after Akaev's visit. Yet the strength of local feeling was such that the president has to replace him with a representative of another powerful local family.[18] Meanwhile Osmanov remained an important actor in the south, elected a parliamentary deputy in February 1995 and allegedly playing a key role in the burgeoning southern drugs trade. The ongoing significance of the north-south divide was also evident in the December 1995 presidential elections when Communist leader Absamat Masaliev officially polled nearly 50% in the southern Osh region, despite the best efforts of the local administration to obstruct his campaign.

Network politics is extremely hard to unravel and its political salience is almost impossible to assess with any degree of conviction. Every so often examples surface, evident in claims that the Republican Peoples Party was essentially a Talas based organisation, though the September 1994 poll quoted earlier revealed no support for the RPP in this region. Others have claimed that, lacking his own patronage network, Askar Akaev coopted that of the Brezhnevite party boss and former political enemy Turdakun Usubaliev, something that enabled him to achieve record electoral support in the Naryn region in December 1995. And when the newspaper *Kriminal* was closed down after only two issues in 1997, one of the articles that gave particular offence had suggested that republican politics was dominated by a Talas-Kemin mafia—Kemin in the Chu region being the birthplace of Akaev and Talas that of his wife. To these geographical ties one should add the often overlapping connections stemming from friendship, marraige or working together in the old Soviet hierarchy. For example, Akaev's continued defence of Dastan Sarygulov, the chairman of the state company and a man frequently charged with corruption or incompetence, is said to stem in part from the fact that the latter was reportedly best man at the president's wedding.[19]

Though Akaev has been increasingly critical of the role of 'tribalism' in Kyrgyz politics, in part its continued strength would appear to stem from his own political strategies. During his early years in power the president built up an alliance with regional bosses, and in particular with the powerful akims or governors of the country's six region who he was responsible for appointing. They utilised their position to aid Akaev in the dissolution of parliament and in ensuring satisfactory results during referenda, and in return enjoyed considerable leeway in the governance of their own territories. Yet this policy only reinforced regionalism, allowing local patronage networks to consolidate and to manipulate political life, in particular at the time of the 1995 parliamentary elections which saw the return of many deputies deemed undesirable by Akaev. During this campaign the contest in many constituencies was based upon a combined appeal to clan loyalties and the utilisation of economic power to make promises to the electorate. And it might be argued that the very nature of transitional politics further strengthened this type of politics, for during times of economic certainty the need for patrons increases amongst the mass of the population, for after all though the relation between patron and client is unequal, it is nonetheless mutually beneficial.[20]

Kyrgyz commentators have offered numerous suggestions as to how tribalism's influence might be curtailed or civilised so as to serve a more modern form of politics. During the early 1990s there were some calls in the south for greater political autonomy, the possible division of the country into two, or the creation of some type of federal system, though there was little evidence that separatism appealed to the mass of the southern population. Various politicians, from radical critic Topchubek Turgunaliev to academician Turar Koichuev have put forward proposals for administrative change. Turgunaliev has suggested a simplification of the republic's administrative structure and a programme of equalisation to ensure that certain regions do not benefit disproportionally from foreign and state credits; Koichuev, writing in 1997, argued for a new appointments structure that would reflect merit and ability rather than belonging. Akaev for his part, appeared in 1996 to begin a process of rotation of cadres, whereby senior officials served as administrators in different regions. The problem with such a policy, as was discoved by Moscow pre-1991, was that officials who stay too long in one region tend to be coopted into local networks whilst those who stay briefly fail to get to grips with the real issues. Equally, when attempts are made to introduce the selection of leaders through the ballot box, it is not difficult in predominantly rural areas for regional bosses to mobilise the vote behind their chosen candidates or ensure that councils of elders are dominated by the 'right' people. However one defines it 'tribalism' is not going to disappear from Kyrgyz life. In the words of one leading journalist it 'was, is and will be'.[21] The real question may be whether it can be rendered 'civil', something Akaev appeared to believe in his early speeches about Kyrgyz tribal democracy but seems far more sceptical about today.[22]

PRESERVING ETHNIC HARMONY

Since the achievement of independence, a major concern of President Akaev has been with the preservation of civic harmony and ethnic peace, an objective that has not always sat easily with the nation building process. At the time of the 1989 census, Kyrgyz had made up just 52% of the population, followed by Russians who made up 22%, Uzbeks 13%, Ukrainians 3%, Tatars and Germans 2% each, with various other groups including Uighurs, Dungans, Tajiks, Kazakhs. These figures in turn disguised regional and occupational variations, with most of the Slavs resident in the northern regions and in the capital, and dominant in administration and industry, and the Uzbeks heavily concentrated in the south and primarily occupied with settled agriculture and handicrafts. As the republic became independent the political elite could not forget how easily bloody inter-communal conflict had developed in the Osh region during 1990, nor be blind to the gradual increase in Russian emigration from the late 1980s onwards. Leaving aside the ethnic question, such developments had practical implications, because the Slavs and Germans still provided many of the skilled professionals essential for Kyrgyzstan's successful short-term transition. For that reason it was not surprising to find Akaev repeatedly stressing his commitment to the creation of a multi-ethnic state to which members of all national groups could feel they belonged. For this reason he vetoed a draft land law that appeared to reserve landownership for ethnic Kyrgyz and offered citizenship to all legally resident in Kyrgyzstan at the time of independence. In speech after speech, Akaev spoke of good relations between ethnic groups as one of his major concerns, and in the early 1990s held a series of meetings with various national cultural centres who in turn committed themselves to work together to preserve civic concord.[23]

In practice the problems for the state raised by different groups varied considerably. The small numbers of Dungans, Uighurs, and Tajiks meant that they were of little consquences for the authorities in pursuing the goal of ethnic harmony though, as we shall see in a later chapter, the treatment of the latter two groups had international ramifications, in the first case for relations with China and in the second creating a substantial refugee problem on Kyrgyz soil. More problematic was the Uzbek population in the south, traumatised by the events of 1990 and suspicious of the authorities in Bishkek. During the post-war era the proportion of the population which was Uzbek had gradually increased, from around 10% in 1939 to over 14% in 1995, and in the two southern oblasts of the country they comprised substantial minorities—just over a quarter in the Osh region and nearly 40% in Jalalabad. Yet despite making up a significant proportion of the population there was a growing perception amongst the Uzbeks that their place in the new Kyrgyzstan remained insecure.

A number of developments reinforced these fears, including the de facto continuation of Turdakun Usubaliev's tendency to reduce the number of Uzbeks in administrative positions. Hence by the mid-1990s Uzbeks held only 4.7% of key posts in the Osh regional administration, only two positions on the Jalalabad town government, and had only six deputies in the country's parliament.[24] There was also a perception that little was being done to meet the cultural and linguistic needs of the minority, with complaints that though Bishkek remained overly sensitive to the Russian language issue, it had refused to grant any official status to Uzbek. Tensions between Kyrgyz and Uzbeks were further exacerbated by differing patterns of socio-economic development, which many of the titular nationality saw as leaving the Uzbeks better placed to take advantage of the new situation. Thus the Uzbek minority tended to dominate in the fields of trade, transport and handicrafts, and to be resident in urban areas where the possibilities of economic activity were greater than in the Kyrgyz dominated and often impoverished rural areas. In consequence, from the 1980s onwards large numbers of Kyrgyz youth had flooded to the towns in search of work. It was such people who had played a key role in the conflicts of 1990 and who many feared might facilitate a repeat of those tragic events.

During the early 1990s, some Uzbeks in the south responded to these problems by supporting moves towards greater autonomy from the capital whilst others pushed for unification with neighbouring Uzbekistan, though territorial claims were eschewed by the latter's president, Islam Karimov. Bishkek's response was largely rhetorical, attacking 'extremists' and stressing its commitment to equality between ethnic groups. In practice the government elite did little beyond encouraging the creation of a Kyrgyz-Uzbek friendship society, and setting up a committee to prepare the celebrations of the forthcoming 3,000th anniversary of the town of Osh. In the south, however, tensions lingered beneath the surface, with surveys carried out in 1995 revealing that over half of Uzbeks in the two regions had recently experienced ethnic hatred and that many believed inter-ethnic clashes were likely in the near future.[25] And at the end of 1997 government fears of Uzbek political organisation were revealed, when the authorities sponsored the creation of a new national cultural centre in the Osh region, a move which some Uzbeks saw as an attempt to develop more effective control over their cultural life.

Whilst Uzbek-Kyrgyz relations perhaps have greater potential for arousing bloody conflict, of greater immediate concern to the authorities has been the retention of the European and Slavic peoples who have played such a key role in administration and economic management. In 1989 there were around 100,000 Germans resident in Kyrgyzstan, most of them the descendants of families deported from the western regions of the USSR after the Nazi invasion in June 1941. By mid-1991 around 15,000 had left for Germany, which offered an open door for all those of proven German descent, and there was increasing concern that many more would leave. Addressing a conference of Kyrgyz Germans held in early 1992 Akaev went out of his way to praise the contribution this community had made to the development of the republic, and defined his chief objective in the sphere of ethnic relations as realising the interests of all ethnic groups within Kyrgyzstan regardless of nationality. He expressed the hope that there would develop a special relationship which brought in the local community and the Federal Republic in support of a continued German presence within the republic. At the end of January 1992 he issued a decree setting up two German National Cultural Districts to be run by elected representatives who would have autonomy to decide economic and social issues. Not all Kyrgyz were happy at what they saw as a renunciation of sovereignty, but Akaev argued that this was a special case and that it was necessary to take special measures to retain the services of this useful minority. At the same time it was hoped that preserving a German community within the republic would serve as a magnet for German investors and financial support from the government in Bonn, which had its own interest in persuading its co-ethnics not to migrate.[26] Nonetheless, by 1997 only around 20,000 remained, and many in the north faced increasing hardship as the industries within which they worked faced restructuring and downsizing. And as numbers fell it became harder to maintain a distinctive cultural identity, especially as many of those remaining were more comfortable in Russian than German, something recognised by a decision of the Lutheran churches in some parts or the republic to start holding services in Russian.

The Kyrgyz leadership has been particularly concerned to meet the needs of the Russian and Russian-speaking population who totalled around a quarter of the population in 1989. From the late 1980s this group experienced, or felt itself to be subject to, increasing pressures within Kyrgyzstan stemming in particular from the growth of nationalism. Central here was the adoption of the state language law in September 1989 which proposed a fairly rapid changeover to the use of Kyrgyz in administration and education. For Russian speakers who had never learnt the local language, and indeed had been unable to, even if willing, after Russian schools ceased teaching Kyrgyz in the 1960s, this law appeared discriminatory. For the elderly there was little prospect of learning a new language, and the time frame within which change was envisaged was unrealistic, even for many Russified Kyrgyz who had little facility in their own language.

Other factors contributed towards the 'social discomfort' of Russians, including the growing nationalist tone of many political activists, the anti-Russian tone given to the 75th anniversary celebrations of the 1916 steppe revolt which were seen as glorifying Kyrgyz resistance and demonising the role of the Russians, the tendency to make political and administrative appointments on the basis of ethnicity and, in the southern regions, a suspicion of the perceived or possible growth of Islamic influences. As the republic moved into its first five years of independence, these fears were exacerbated by the increasing dominance of Kyrgyz in business, administration and political life, with 85% of local deputies elected in 1984 coming from the titular nationality and 84% in the 1995 parliamentary elections.

The most immediate response to these developments was emigration, with many Russian speakers leaving the republic during the early 1990s (see Table 2). More importantly many of these were highly skilled professionals whom the republic needed, including many academics, teachers, and over 1,000 doctors. Asked in a 1992 survey why they would consider leaving, most Russians pointed to the worsening of inter-ethnic relations (59.7%) and the adoption of laws that discriminated against Russians (29.4%), though some cited other factors including the poor economic situation (13.5%), fear of unemployment (7.6%), price rises (6.6%), fear of physical violence (13.2%) and concern that their children would not get a proper education in the new republic (16.5%). Above all there seemed to be a fear that whatever the good intentions of Akaev and other members of the republican elite, future generations would be less accomodating and that therefore the prospects for Russians in the next century would be increasingly poor.[27] Though the authorities, including Akaev, suggested that economic motives underlay emigration, it was clear from these and other sociological surveys that the perception that Russians were not wanted motivated many to consider leaving. Of course emigration was not an option for some, especially the elderly, the unskilled, and those with no real roots outside the republic. Some who did leave found it hard to adapt to life in Russia and later returned to Kyrgyzstan.

Table 2:   Distribution by selected nationalities of those leaving the
Kyrgyz Republic in 1989–96

	1989	1990	1991	1992	1993	1994	1995	1996
Number leaving*	60815	82852	71315	103728	143619	71197	37302	27584
Russians	1328	32893	32032	59294	89984	41463	18718	14020
% of those leaving	35.1	39.7	44.9	57.2	62.7	58.2	50.2	50.8
Ukrainians	2734	4484	4178	8064	11740	5267	2742	1773
%	4.5	5.4	5.9	7.8	8.2	7.4	6.6	6.5
Belarussians	284	292	342	722	885	366	177	117
%	0.5	0.4	0.5	0.7	0.6	0.5	0.5	0.4
Germans	16498	17094	14278	12833	11148	8236	6070	4039
%	27.1	20.6	20	12.4	7.8	11.6	16.3	14.7
Jews	298	1044	611	489	637	467	323	235
%	0.5	1.3	0.9	0.5	0.4	0.7	0.9	0.9
Tatars	2224	2898	2311	4286	9486	4128	1941	1392
%	3.7	3.5	3.2	4.1	6.6	5.8	5.2	5

* ignores the fact there there was also some immigration during these years, though at relatively low levels
(Source: adapted from *Sotsial'no-ekonomicheskie problemy migratsii naseleniia kyrgyzskoi respubliki, 1991-96gg.* Bishkek, Kyrgyz-Russian Slavonic University, 1997, pp. 85–6)

Amongst those who stayed there were considerable debates over how to handle the new situation in which they found themselves. In the south the reaction of many Slavs was to opt for passivity and a quiet life. Monitors during the February 1995 parliamentary elections observed that in the southern oblasts whole streets and apartment blocks of Russians did not participate in the vote. In the northern regions, especially in the capital Bishkek, and in Chu and Talas oblasts the situation was more complex for in many areas Russians made up the majority of the population. The more radical activists joined groups such as the Semirechie Cossacks who fought a continuing struggle for recognition with the authorities and whose meetings were sometimes accompanied by calls for a reconstitution of a greater Russia, something hardly likely to endear them to the new state. Other groups such as the Slavic Fund and Soglasie (Agreement) operated on the principle that Russians had a future in Kyrgyzstan, and concentrated their efforts on improving the rights of this particular group. During 1994 such groups argued for various policy shifts that might encourage Russian speakers to stay, including the introduction of dual citizenship, a change in the status of the Russian language, the stabilisation of the socio-economic situation and stronger guarantees for the rights of ethnic minorities. Prior to the 1995 parliamentary elections Soglasie declared its intention to back candidates from any ethnic group who would defend the interests of ethnic Russians, seek changes on the question of the status of Russian language and Slavic access to economic resources through privatisation. Yet by 1996 the Slavic Fund was to be found criticising the five Russian deputies for their inability to defend Russian interests. And though they accepted that the rights of Russians were defended better here than elsewhere in Central Asia, Slavic activists claimed that the team around the president was inclined to an increasingly ethnocratic policy which turned a blind eye to abuses of minority rights.

Probably the key issue affecting the Russians in Kyrgyzstan has been the status of the Russian language. During the debate over the adoption of a new constitution in 1992–3 this question came to the fore, as both Russians and many Kyrgyz argued for a reconsideration of the issue. Of particular concern was the target date of 1994 set for speaking Kyrgyz in all administrative and education institutions, a goal which critics charged was physically impossible to meet given the inadequate facilities available for the study of the state language. By February 1993 the parliamentary commission drafting the new constitution had received over 200 letters concerning the language issue, some of which had been published in the press. Many repeated the argument about the timetable and discriminatory aspects of the existing situation, and reinforced this with pragmatic arguments which pointed to the role of Russian as an international language, the absence of Kyrgyz versions of many key scientific texts, and the need to encourage Russians to stay in the republic. Others suggested that Kyrgyzstan could follow the example of other states and have two or more official languages. Few concessions were finally made, with the proposal to have Russian described as the language of 'inter-ethnic communication' rejected as legally meaningless, though there was some tightening of the constitutional guarantees for those using languages other than Kyrgyz.[28]

Yet though Akaev suspended implementation of the language law in 1993, the issue would not go away and further discussion took place as emigration reached record proportions in that year. Alarmed by this the authorities sought ways to stem the flow, and in June 1994 convened a major round table conference on the theme 'Russians in Kyrgyzstan'. Addressing this gathering Akaev noted that continued good relations with Russia were overshadowed by declining trade relations and tensions over the situation of Russians within the republic. To this end he argued for moves to strengthen the structures of civil society so as to allow Russian organisations to make their voices heard, and for the development of greater cooperation in economic ventures of various types. Shortly after this gathering the president issued a decree 'on regulating migratory processes in the Kyrgyz republic' which allowed Russian to be used in those institutions and areas where Slavs formed a majority and in scientific fields where Russian was the normal language of exchange, and which promised greater efforts to ensure the just representation of non-Kyrgyz in the selection of leading officials. He also proposed a reconsideration of the language and electoral laws and, after the 1995 elections produced a predominantly Kyrgyz assembly, suggested that some thought might be given to ethnic quotas in future parliamentary elections. Alongside this Akaev's decree enjoined the security agencies to pay greater attention to monitoring extreme nationalist outbursts, with prosecutions to be more vigorously pursued than at present. Finally, the document stressed the need to develop citizenship treaties with Russia as soon as possible so as to regulate the flow of people between the two republics. In later years this decree was to be credited with slowing down the rate of migration, but though it may have had some impact, the subsequent reduction in numbers leaving probably had more to do with the fact that many of those remaining lacked the opportunity to depart.

In December 1994 Akaev raised the language issue at a constitutional convention called to rethink certain aspects of the 1993 constitution and argued that though the position of Kyrgyz language as the state language should be retained, some modification of policy was essential. Debate continued over the next two years, and in early 1996 the Constitutional Court approved in principle a change to Article 5-2 of the Constitution so as to read 'in the Kyrgyz Republic Russian may be used as an official language'. Despite Akaev's support for this change, as of mid-1997 the issue had still not been finally settled and many Russians remained unhappy, suspecting that this stalling represented a reluctance on the part of many Kyrgyz to take their needs seriously. Equally amongst the Kyrgyz there was considerable ambiguity amongst legislators with an issue that had taken on many resonances beyond the narrowly linguistic. In particular, many legislators felt that only by protecting the status of the Kyrgyz language could any sense of national, as opposed to regional identity, be developed and reinforced. Thus even in parliament many of the more Russified deputies were highly critical of any infringement on the position of the state language though, as one critic pointed out, at least one defender of the state language still hedged his bets by sending his children to Russian speaking schools. Yet for all these problems and the very real suspicion that the republic was pursuing an increasingly ethnocentric policy in many areas, Russians remain in a better position here than elsewhere in Central Asia and the Russian language remains the primary means of communication within the republic, especially in the north and amongst the administrative elite.

ELECTIONS AND CONSTITUTIONAL CHANGE

Following the October 1994 referendum, President Akaev convened a constitutional gathering to discuss further changes to the Kyrgyz political system. In an effort to ensure, or give the impression of proper representation, this body was to be made up of representatives of the various regional and sectional interests in society. These were to include leading political figures such as the president, parliamentary speaker, prime minister, 35 representatives from each oblast and from the capital, 35 from the Assembly of the Peoples of Kyrgyzstan—a talking shop in which representatives of different nationalities were able to express their concerns and defend their interests—15 from political parties, 15 from trade unions, and 10 each from agrarian organisations, businessmen, young people, women, veterans and creative artists.

Addressing this gathering Akaev appeared to step back from his earlier enthusiasm for liberal democracy, suggesting that the simple application of Western style parliamentarianism might be inappropriate in the Central Asian context. In the West this form of rule was based upon a strong economy in which clearly defined property relations helped to shape distinctive class and social interests. In addition there was to be found a mature civil society and strong institutional structures supported by a democratic political culture and well developed political parties. All of these things were lacking in Kyrgyzstan where the advocates of reform had to battle against strongly entrenched group interests based upon the old party system and traditional clan structures, where corruption was rife, and where the opposition was inclined to a destructive criticism that added little to political life. Above all the state remained weak and unable to tackle the serious and mounting problems facing the country. In such circumstances there was a need for a lengthier transition period than had been anticipated, an era of proto-democracy during which all spheres of public life would be subject to an evolutionary process of democratisation. In this period it was essential to strengthen the power and capability of the state and Akaev argued that this required some rethinking of the balance of power between executive and legislature. At the same time he repeated his call for a re-assessment of current policies in the controversial areas of land reform—where he favoured a move towards private ownership—and the issue of the state language. One month later draft constitutional amendments were published which clearly shifted power in the direction of the president, who was now given the right to 'determine major trends in the state's foreign and domestic policy', formerly a parliamentary right, and which removed the need for parliamentary approval of individual ministers who would now be appointed by the prime minister. Yet though these were subject to some discussion, the question of constitutional reform was temporarily shelved as parliamentary elections were called, initially for 24 December and then postponed until 5 February 1995.

These elections were called to fill places in the new, two-chamber parliament created as a result of the October referendum. The upper house, or People's Assembly, was to be made up of seventy deputies who would meet several times a year to discuss the general direction of Kyrgyz policy, whilst the smaller 35 seat Legislative Assembly was to be the functioning legislature which met regularly in a law making capacity. Elections to these bodies were to be based on two groups of single member constituencies. Under the terms of a hastily issued electoral law, victory in the campaign required that candidates achieved an absolute majority of the vote on a 50% turnout. Failing this the two leading candidates would go forward to a run off ballot two weeks later and, if this failed to produce a result, then new elections would be held from which previous candidates would be barred. The right to nominate candidates was given to registered political parties, work collectives and public meetings of electors in their place of residence—the latter two cases easily subject to manipulation by regional bosses. Each candidacy had to be verified by local electoral commissions though, if an individual was rejected, they could appeal to the Central Electoral Commission.

In practice the election campaign was accompanied by numerous abuses as a large number of candidates contested the field, many of them individuals with doubtful records who utilised their resources to ensure election to positions where they would enjoy some immunity from prosecution. According to one report nearly a third of those eventually elected were at the time being officially investigated for illegal financial dealings. During the nomination campaign there were many complaints about the activitites of local electoral commissions, said to be in the hands of the authorities or of regional bosses. Yet at one point over 1,000 candidates were registered of whom 936 eventually contested the 105 available seats. Of these around 160 were proposed by political parties, but most represented local administrators, emerging business groups, or those tied into familial or nomenklatura groupings—often overlapping categories. In general their programmes were indistinguishable, offering populist appeals with little substantial content. Thus Suleiman Imanbaev standing in Tokmak spoke of the need to offer better social protection for those impoverished by reform but offered no ideas as to how this was to be achieved, whilst Radyk Shekinov a former health minister stood on the slogan 'Democracy is order, order is democracy', and proposed the execution of virtually all murderers and rapists, and increasing prison sentences for a wide variety of offences.[29]

Figure 1: Poster calling on electors to take part in the parliamentary elections of February 1995, reading 'People of Kyrgyzstan! The future of the republic – in your hands'.

On election day there was considerable effort to achieve a high turnout as the media and local authorities encouraged people to vote (see Figure 1). At the same time numerous abuses were recorded as fathers voted for whole families, regional bosses sent minders to 'observe' elections or to offer scarce goods for sale outside polling booths, and many counts were not adequately verified by the relevant electoral commissions. Officially the turnout was recorded at 76.25% but because of the large number of candidates only 16 deputies were elected at the first ballot, including the writer Chingiz Aitmatov, two former Communist Party bosses Turdakun Usubaliev and Absamat Masaliev, and Omurbek Tekebaev leader of the moderate nationalist party Ata meken. Two weeks later a second ballot brought the total number of deputies to around 90, though some results were the subject of numerous appeals and reconsideration by the Central Electoral Commission, whilst the remaining seats had to be filled in repeat elections during subsequent months.

Of the 105 deputies eventually elected 87 were ethnic Kyrgyz, a substantial over-representation, and only 5 were women (reduced to 4 when one accepted a ministerial post in early 1996). Around 20 had been members of the old parliament and just under 40 were reported to have some party affiliation, though in most cases this was fairly loose. Few of the parties had made much impact, with the well-organised Communist Party acquiring just 3 deputies, and only the Social Democratic Party of Kyrgyzstan (SDPK), with its strong roots amongst regional administrators and the new business class, able to make a substantial impact with 14 deputies. The smaller nationalist parties did badly and no party other than the SPDK gained more than 4 seats. The elections also represented a rebuff to President Akaev insofar as many candidates suspected of financial impropriety were able to gain election and in many areas voters returned local bosses in preference to officials placed there by the centre. Speaking after the event the president claimed that the existing election law allowed members of the old elite and representatives of criminal groups to be successful. In such circumstances he felt it might be necessary to redesign the electoral process for future contests.[30] For a few days there were rumours that Akaev had considered declaring the elections invalid, but he soon proclaimed himself committed to working with the new parliament and expressed the hope that it would make a constructive contribution to the reform process.

Such optimism was to prove shortlived as the two chambers of parliament embarked upon a bitter dispute over their respective spheres of influence—a tension maintained over the next two years and one which would occasionally see loyalty to chamber over-ride loyalty to region. The problem stemmed in part from Akaev's calling of elections to a two-chamber parliament despite the fact that the functioning 1993 constitution made no provision for such a body. Particularly galling for the president was parliament's persistent failure to swear in a constitutional court because the People's Assembly and the Legislative Assembly could not agree whose prerogative this was. And without a constitutional court the president could get no ruling on the wider constitutional changes he hoped to push through. The Legislative Assembly also created future problems for itself when a majority, but not the necessary absolute majority, elected M. Cholponbaev as speaker, a man who would later be forced to resign following allegations of financial improprieties. Akaev became increasingly disenchanted with this squabbling parliament and, in consequence, gave discrete encouragement to those deputies who proposed holding a referendum on extending the presidential term as had recently happened in Uzbekistan and Kazakhstan. In August 1995 a petitition with around one million signatures purporting to support this proposal was presented, though many of the signatures appeared to have been falsified and the Legislative Assembly meeting in September simply rejected it. In response to this rebuff Akaev announced that given the ongoing controversy he would bring forward presidential elections, due in 1996, to 24 December 1995 a move reluctantly agreed by the Legislative Assembly though 12 of its 35 deputies walked out rather than vote.

Potential opponents of Akaev were extremely critical of the short time period allowed for the campaign arguing that this would deny them the opportunity to gain the requisite 50,000 signatures or to put together a proper campaign. Moreover, opponents faced considerable opposition in some areas where regional administrators acted to prevent the collection or deny the verification of signatures. By early December six candidates were registered: Askar Akaev, former parliamentary speaker Medetkhan Sherimkulov, Communist leader Absamat Masaliev, former Communist leader Jumgalbek Amanbaev, leader of the Ata meken party Omurbek Tekebaev, and the recently dismissed director of a southern factory Mamat Aybalaev. Then with just nine days to go the Central Electoral Commission announced that the registration of the last three had been removed for violations of the electoral law relating to the collection of signatures—something of which all candidates were probably guilty. Moreover, the election campaign was becoming increasingly one-sided as most of the mass media campaigned overtly for Akaev, with *Slovo kyrgyzstana* publishing pages of endorsements from well know Kyrgyz public figures, religious leaders and CIS heads of state. Further problems affected the campaign of Sherimkulov as his campaign manager Topchubek Turgunaliev was arrested and charged with fomenting ethnic hatred between Kazakhs and Kyrgyz. On election day itself more irregularities were reported, though the Central Electoral Commission claimed an 86.19% turnout amongst the electorally fatigued Kyrgyz. Of these 71.59% were said to have voted for the incumbent. Although opponents claimed considerable degrees of fraud—evident for example in the report of one journalist that his father had died in August 1995 but voted for the president in December—it may well be that the result reflected a traditional inclination to back existing leaders. When the voting patterns are examined more closely considerable regional variations become apparent, with Akaev gaining 97% of the vote in the Naryn region, whilst being run very close in the southern Osh region where Absamat Masaliev officially took 46.53% of the vote despite the best efforts of the presidentially appointed administrator. Thus whilst the contest hardly conformed to best democratic practice, its result, like that of its parliamentary predecessor, was not entirely unreflective of the existing balance of political forces within the country.

However unsatisfactory the exercise, Akaev utilised this renewed legitimacy to call for a further extension of presidential powers, claiming that at present he had no more powers than the Queen of England. In early January he published a series of proposals for constitutional change, including giving the head of state the power to appoint and retire members of the government, to appoint judges at all levels and, with the approval of parliament, to make other key appointments. Though parliamentary approval was still required for the choice of prime minister, if parliament rejected the president's choice three times he could dissolve the legislature. All of this was justified on the grounds that deputies had persistently failed to get on with the task of creating a legislative basis for the creation of a market economy, instead preferring to focus on laws defining their own privileges. Critics countered that such changes, taken together with growing pressure on the media and the arrest of several oppositionists, heralded a slide towards dictatorship. Supporters of Akaev disagreed, claiming that he still enjoyed less personal power than most other CIS leaders and stressing that parliamentary laws still remained constitutionally superior to presidential decrees. Whatever the arguments, the amended constitution was put to an electorally weary population on 10 February 1996 who responded with a Soviet style 96.5% turnout of whom 94.5% supported the proposed changes. Armed with these new powers Akaev moved to make changes in other disputed areas, helping to push through changes regarding the constitutional status of the Russian language which he proposed should became an official language of the Kyrgyz republic and, in November 1996, signing a decree effectively permitting private ownership of land from the beginning of 1997. None of these measures satisfied the critics in parliament and outside, but despite the doubts of many deputies and the more limited powers available to parliament, the Legislative Assembly did appear to adopt a more constructive approach to policy making and proved willing to process a far greater volume of legislation in 1996 and 1997 than in previous years.

TOWARDS BENEVOLENT AUTHORITARIANISM?

Following this series of flawed elections and constitutional changes pushed through by the president, some critics charged that Akaev was reverting to Central Asian type, with a thin veneer of democratic rhetoric and practice disguising more authoritarian forms of rule. Presidential impatience with democratic norms were first alluded to in mid-1994 when Akaev attacked certain sections of the media for their irresponsibility and suggested that the parliamentary paper *Svobodny gory* should be closed down by the courts after it published what he described as anti-semitic attacks on one of his chief advisers. One month later a Bishkek district court closed the paper down, claiming that the paper 'had systematically published deliberately false information in its pages aimed at discrediting state bodies and legitimate state power in the person of the president'. At the same time Akaev issued a decree creating a public chamber for media activity which stressed the need for a responsible media, though this body was formally to be independent of governmental control and included amongst its members respected figures such as V. Niksdorf the parliamentary correspondent of *Slovo kyrgyzstana*. At the end of that year Akaev ordered the reinstatement of the parliamentary paper, albeit under closer scrutiny, but it was clear that he was not happy with what he saw as the overly critical stance of some papers. During 1995 it was the turn of the often acerbic *Res publika* whose critical stance and exposure of corruption had offended many in high office. In March 1995 Akaev sued the paper for suggesting he had real estate in Turkey and Switzerland and its editors were given one year suspended sentences and banned from working as journalists for 18 months, the latter sentence having little legal basis according to their defence attorney.

This growing pressure on the media reflected various concerns on the part of the political elite. Whilst there was a genuine fear that an excessively critical media and opposition would serve to undermine what was seen as very vulnerable civic harmony, there were also many within the elite who had little commitment to political pluralism or a free press and would have preferred a reversion to the older styles of rule. In addition there were some popular pressures from a people with little experience of democracy and a certain wariness of the new world in which their children were subject to a wide variety of undesirable pressures, from pornography, through drug abuse to seduction by 'undesirable' religious groups. In such circumstances pressures from parts of the elite were often reinforced by a public opinion suspicious of change or diversity, which thus provided at least some constituency of support for a restoration of 'law and order'. This change in atmosphere led many leading newspapers to adopt a more cautious approach, as the legacy of seventy years of censorship reasserted itself.[31]

One area where this growing suspicion of pluralism became apparent during the mid-1990s was in the field of religious life. Throughout the country foreign based groups, from Protestant missionaries to Islamic activists from Pakistan and elsewhere, set up their own communities, provided financial support for local groups and engaged in proselytising activities. In mid-1995 the Kyrgyz security services warned about the activities of foreign groups encouraging Islamic 'fundamentalism' in the southern regions, and from the end of 1995 the authorities began to speak of the need to keep a closer watch on religious life. In mid-1996 a government body to monitor religious activity was set up—headed by Emilbek Kaptagaev—and religious education was banned in state schools. Alongside this there was growing debate in the media over how to handle religion, with some calling for a complete ban on the activities of foreign groups. As in Russia some of the pressure for change came from the Muslim and Orthodox communities who often lacked the financial resources and activist tradition of many of the foreign missionaries. Il'ias Nazarbekov, head of the external affairs department of the Kyrgyz muftiate, expressed concern that some of these groups were dividing families, using money and psychological pressure to win converts, and then encouraging them not to serve in the army. Implicitly rejecting the notion of freedom of choice, he went on to suggest that all Kyrgyz should by rights be Muslims and all Russians Orthodox.

By the end of 1996 some of these concerns were being taken up by the authorities, with the Ministry of Justice calling for a re-registration of religious communities and President Akaev issuing a temporary decree on the registration of foreign groups. During a press conference to announce this measure Kaptagaev stressed that the activities of religious organisations must conform to the law and the needs of state security, though in a later interview with the author he suggested that the re-registration process was largely a routine accounting measure and a means of ensuring order in the religious sphere. Some Kyrgyz were less convinced by such developments, seeing them as marking a return to Soviet era policies of control over religious life.[32] This view appeared to be confirmed at the end of 1996 when the authorities supported the efforts of groups within the Muslim community who wanted to remove the sitting mufti. On the grounds that the 1993 kurultai (council) of Muslims had been subject to legal irregularities the Muslim establishment was deprived of its registration by the Ministry of Justice, and a new kurultai was called at which a mufti more acceptable to the authorities was elected.[33] Yet it should be stressed that many Kyrgyz citizens, both in local commun-ities where there was religious competition and amongst some otherwise lib-eral intellectuals, felt that there was a need for tighter control over religious life and that traditional groups were subject to unfair competitition from well financed missionaries of all sorts. By late 1997, despite Akaev's rejection of a return to 'administrative measures in the religious sphere',[34] there was some discussion of the need for a new law on religion which would bring order into a sphere of life with potentially divisive consequences for the new republic.

Alongside debates over religious freedom and growing pressures on the media characterised by the removal of editors in some cases and a growing trend to self-censorship by the state run papers, came more direct pressure on opposition activists. In the period 1995–7 a number were subject to legal proceedings, ostensibly on the grounds of their criminal activities rather than political opposition. During the 1995 presidential campaign Topchubek Turgunaliev and Jumagaz Usupov, both supporting the candidacy of former speaker Medetkhan Sherimkulov, were arrested for allegedly distributing leaflets slandering Akaev. In his defence speech Turgunaliev pointed out that no witnesses had seen him give out the offending literature, and claimed that it could not be described as slanderous to say that Akaev had presided over a period of economic decline. Given a one year sentence, the defendants were immediately released and, in his usual uninhibited fashion, Turgunaliev returned to the fray. Keeping up his criticism of the government, and con-tributing to a further split within his own party, in November 1996 he was instrumental, together with former Communist leader Jumgalbek Amanbaev, in forming a new social movement entitled 'for deliverance from poverty'.[35] On 17 December this movement picketed the government building demand-ing recompense for those who had lost their savings when a leading bank had collapsed earlier that year. During the course of that day Turgunaliev was arrested, allegedly for failing to turn up at a pre-arranged trial scheduled for the previous day. The charges on this occasion dated back to when he was dean of Bishkek's humanitarian university and his co-defendant Timur Stam-kulov was commercial director. According to the defence Stamkulov bor-rowed $10,000 from the university and this was approved by Turgunaliev, after which Stamkulov was robbed en route to pay back the loan. The authorities, however, accused the two of embezzlement despite the fact that the existing head of the university stated that his institution had no financial claims against the two. Whatever the facts of the case it is hard to see that they merited prosecution under criminal rather than civil law or that justice was being seen to be done in Kyrgyzstan. Critics also pointed out that a meeting of the state Security Council in September had led to the sacking of some officials and the reprimand of others for embezzling many times more than the accused, yet noted that none these officials had been brought to trial. Turgunaliev and Stamkulov were less fortunate, the former sentenced to ten years imprisonment and the confiscation of his property and the latter to six years. Though the sentences were later reduced, with Turgunaliev receiving four years, he was immediately sent to an isolated penal colony in the south where he remained until Hilary Clinton's trip to Bishkek in November 1997 after which he was brought back to a less rigourous internment in the capital.

For many critics the trial of Turgunaliev was seen as heralding a new wave of pressure on the opposition and critical outlets within the media. At the beginning of 1997 the paper *Kriminal* was launched, but after two issues it was closed down by the Ministry of Justice for allegedly insulted key officials. Simultaneously leading officials became bolder in attacking the media, with one factory director successfully pressing charges against journalist Yrsybek Omurzakov after he took up the cases of abused employees— a charge which in the autumn of 1997 led to the writer being sentenced to thirty months imprisonment. At the same time the director of the state gold company Dastan Sarygulov took the editor and certain journalists on *Res publika* to court in May 1997, alleging libel. As a result of this case the paper's editor Zamira Sydykova and journalist Aleksandr Alianchikov were sentenced to 18 months, and two other writers were ordered not to engage in journalism for 18 months. Though the sentences for the first two were later reduced and those of the latter over-ruled by the courts, even many who saw the journalists as guilty of libel felt that the use of the criminal law against them represented an attack on press freedom. This image of a new repressiveness was reinforced by a concurrent press campaign against the local branch of the Soros Foundation which was accused of being too sympathetic to opposition papers, though some 90% of its funding was spent on educational activities. In this atmosphere it was perhaps not surprising to see deputies becoming less respectful of journalists' rights, with frequent attacks by deputies on 'irresponsible' newspapers', and in May 1997 the Legislative Assembly voted to withdraw the accreditation of a number of parliamentary correspondents who they judged too critical.

For some this new authoritarian turn stemmed from Akaev's growing impatience with democracy's ability to get things done and awareness that even a strong commitment to pluralistic politics would provide only marginal benefits in terms of Western aid and support. Others felt that he was under pressure from many within the elite who had little sympathy with democratic politics. Whilst this version was convenient for the presidential team, who some argued were more manipulative than they appeared,[36] it was also in part a consequence of Akaev's political style. Having sought to build up alliances with regional bosses and important bureaucratic and economic actors, he became in part their prisoner and could do little to stop them acting with impunity in their own fiefs. This was particularly evident in his efforts to establish the rule of law, for many leading figures clearly felt themselves to be above the law. In May 1997 the Issyk Kul regional council rejected a procuracy request and voted not to allow its former chairman to be prosecuted, a move that reinforced perceptions that officials were subject to different laws than citizens. By August 1997 the Procuracy was claiming that there were over 100 deputies at all levels, including 8 in the country's parliament, who could not be prosecuted because the respective legislatures would not remove their immunity.[37] In the capital there may have been more pressures to act within the framework of the law, yet there was increasing public suspicion of a legal system that offered more protection to the powerful than the people. Hence the campaign for 'order' in Bishkek, instigated by the new town procurator Marat Kenjakunov, was described by human rights activists as essentially designed to curb opposition. A man who had twice lost his job for abuse of power during the Soviet era and once again under Akaev, he was nevertheless brought back to head the capital's procuracy in 1996, allegedly as a result of his friendship with Akaev's brother. During the first half of 1997 it appears to have been Kenjakunov who led the campaign against Turgunaliev, and who instigated the cases against editors and journalists working for *Res publika*. And it was under his guidance that the town militia utilised considerable brutality against demonstrators protesting the imprisonment of the journalists or picketing on behalf of *Yntymak* movement.

Any assessment of Kyrgyz political life during the 1990s must offer an ambiguous conclusion. On the one hand the country, and especially Bishkek, enjoyed a considerable degree of social pluralism. Social organisations flourished and multiplied, though many survived only for short lengths of time. Despite the harassment of individual papers there remained a considerable degree of press freedom when compared to neighbouring states; religious groups were still free to organise, and for many Western and Eastern based groups and cults there was more scope for action than in most other CIS states. Alongside this, and despite continuing tensions over key appointments, ethnic harmony had been more or less maintained, with no major outbreaks of bloodletting and the scale of emigration dramatically reduced. Yet below the surface how much had changed and was it possible to speak of political as opposed to social pluralism? Political parties proliferated but none had really taken root, except the backwarding looking Communist Party; elections and referenda had been held but to varying degrees these had been manipulated by the centre or regional authorities; informal networks continued to dominate much of political and economic life.

During these years the position and goals of President Akaev have not always been clear. He continued to speak the language of democracy, but the possibility of a genuinely democratic turnover in government looked as distant as ever. Also evident from his speeches was a growing impatience with the opposition and critical media outlets. Nonetheless, there were some signs that, despite the problems, he maintained a commitment to reform. Thus his seemingly undemocratic rejection of the election of local governors can in part be explained by a fear of the further dissipation of power to regional cliques who would control any such elections. And though his administration presided over the increasing harassment of the paper *Asaba* in November 1997, one month later Akaev was to veto a highly restrictive law on the mass media earlier approved by parliament. Against this, one should note that Akaev did little to discourage a moderate but growing personality cult, and that in late 1997 rumours were circulating that some within the presidential apparat were seeking to find a way round the constitutional limit of two presidential terms by holding some form of popular referendum on the extension of Akaev's period in office.

Further problems for the reform process stemmed from the attitude of both elites and masses. Some within the political and commercial elite, remained sceptical of the direction the country was taking, believing that a firm hand was necessary to preserve stability in the long run. Many disliked an openness that allowed their activities to be investigated by the media and discussed by the public at large. Particularly concerned were members of the new rich, in most cases from the old Communist elite, but also including regional bosses and self-made men who had done well in the new system. Such people had sought to anchor themselves in Kyrgyz society by gaining election to parliament or local councils, or by making generous donations for the construction of schools, hospitals or mosques. At the same time, they had used their position in elected bodies to gain immunity from prosecution, and for this reason were keen to impose limits on the activities of the newspapers which publicised their criminal activities. Others in the political elite were critical of the new system for more pragmatic reasons, men like Temirkbek Akmataliev, the akim of Ala-Buka district in Jalalabad region. In an interview given in December 1997 he described himself as 'a convinced believer in dictatorship, albeit temporary until the construction of a strong market economy'. Like many intellectuals in the country his perception was that the country had got its priorities wrong, and that democracy was impossible before the construction of an economic order that benefitted the mass of the population.[38]

This population was one that had largely been passed by during the reform process. Their experience during the 1990s had been a growing impoverishment which contrasted sharply with the lifestyles of the new rich. At the same time democracy had brought little change to the power relationships that had dominated the lives of Kyrgyz citizens in most of the country. Rural dwellers remained dependent upon local bosses and had to vote for them or their proteges in the various elections during the 1990s. In practice, however, the electorate had grown sceptical about the value of their new political rights by the middle of the decade, as was evident at the end of 1997 when a by-election in Bishkek, where there was less possibility of mobilisation by powerful patrons, twice failed to produce the necessary turnout to elect a parliament deputy. Disillusionment was reinforced by the growth of corruption which extended far beyond the scope of the Communist period—as one taxi driver told me, 'at least in the old days there was a fixed level of "rewards" depending upon your rank in the party, but now it is grab what you can so long as you don't get caught'. This growing scepticism about political change was exacerbated by the development of an ideological vacuum that many felt was leaving the Kyrgyz people with no sense of identity or morality. Kyrgyz scholars and politicians might speak approvingly of the role of the Manas epic in developing 'the universal ideas of fraternity, interaction, national pride and independence', but celebration of Manas 'did not put bread on the table'.[39]

Given the context these ambiguities and problems are hardly surprising. This is a region with a strong authoritarian tradition, and one that has been reinforced by seventy years of state socialism. The new Kyrgyz state inherited a serious situation of economic decline and potential ethnic conflict to which most of its neighbours responded by adopting authoritarian styles of rule. Moreover it rules a country with strong regionalist traditions which cannot easily be contained or 'tamed' through electoral systems susceptible to manipulation by local bosses. Although some writers point to the innate democratic tendencies of nomadic cultures which have created some basis for the emergence of genuinely civic traditions—and most visitors are struck by the openness and civility of the Kyrgyz population—their potentiality has been severely constrained by this larger and generally inhospitable context. In such circumstances the observer has to note both the limitations of Kyrgyz politics, when judged by the standards of Western models of liberal democracy, but also to note the achievements in terms of social pluralism and hope that these will not only survive but also that some day they will lay the basis for the creation of a more open polity capable of meeting the political and economic aspirations of the mass of the population.

1   *Slovo Kyrgyzstana* 30 October 1991.
2   *Slovo Kyrgyzstana* 12 December 1991.
3   *Slovo Kyrgyzstana* 2 June 1992.
4   E. Huskey, 'The rise of contested politics in Central Asia: elections in Kyrgyzstan, 1989–90', *Europe-Asia Studies*, 47: 5, 1995, pp. 809–29.
5   This question of whether the new state should develop some form of official ideology or doctrine has been the subject of considerable debate within Kyrgyzstan. In conversation with several Kyrgyz I have been told that the moral problems facing the republic stem from the loss of ideology, and it has been suggested that whilst Communism may have been corrupt, at least it held out some values to growing generation who now are raised to believe in nothing. For a discussion of this issue see Ch. T. Nusupov, *Natsional'naia ideologiia i sovremennost'* (Bishkek, 1997).
6   The text can be found in *Slovo Kyrgyzstana* 21 May 1993.
7   *Slovo Kyrgyzstana* 30 July 1994.
8   *Slovo Kyrgyzstana* 4 April 1991.
9   Interview with Cholponkul Arabaev, Deputy Minister of Justice responsible for the registration of social organisations, 9 September 1997.
10 The capital's main evening paper *Vechernii Bishkek* provided considerable coverage of the movement during the first half of 1997, the hastily erected houses of whose activists were demolished by the militia in the summer and which was denied registration by the Justice Ministry in October.
11 See UNDP, *Directory of Women's Organisations in Central Asia* (Bishkek, 1996), and the critical article in *Vechernii Bishkek* 1 August 1997.
12 The concept of civil society has been the subject of considerable debate amongst Western social scientists with political scientists tended to adopt relatively narrow definitions and anthropologists willing to extend the notion to incorporate 'actually existing civil society' in traditional societies. Cf. L. Diamond, 'Rethinking civil society: towards democratic consolidation', in *Journal of Democracy*, 5: 3, 1994, pp. 4–17, and C. Hann & E. Dunn, ed., *Civil Society: Challenging Western Models* (London, 1996).
13 The law on freedom of conscience and religious organisations approved in late 1991 clearly emphasised the equality of all religious groups and the separation of religion from the state. The text can be found in *Slovo Kyrgyzstana* 13 February 1992.
14 See *Renassans ili regress* (Bishkek, Kyrgyz Peace Research Centre, 1996), especially the first two parts.
15 This about turn has been explained by reference to his presidential ambitions, the discovery of drugs in his parliamentary flat, and allegations concerning his brother's connection with the narco-mafia.
16 *Slovo Kyrgyzstana* 14 February 1995.
17 *Nezavisimaia gazeta* 2.3.1993.
18 *Nezavisimaia gazeta* 28 October 1992.
19 Z. Sydykova, *Za kulisami demokratii po-kyrgyzskii* (Bishkek, 1997), p. 129; it should of course be noted that Sydykova was briefly imprisoned following allegations of libel against Sarygulov and is perhaps not the most objective source.
20 On this point see the discussion in L. Roniger, 'The comparative study of clientelism and the changing nature of civil society in the contemporary world', in L. Roniger, ed., *Democracy, Clientelism and Civil Society* (Boulder & London, Lynne Reinner, 1994), pp. 1–18.
21 Interview with K. Karabekov, deputy political editor of *Vechernii Bishkek*, 8 September 1997.

22 On the possibility of 'civilising tribalism' see R. Achylova, 'Political culture and foreign policy in Kyrgyzstan', in V. Tismaneau, ed., *Political Culture and Civil Society in Russia and the New States of Eurasia*, (New York, M.E. Sharpe, 1995), pp. 318–36.

23 For a discussion of the government's attitude see M. Jangaracheva, 'Rol' natsional'no-kul'turnykh ob'edinenii v stabilizatsii mezhetnicheskikh otnoshenii', in *Renassans ili regress*, pp. 82–87.

24 *Renassans ili regress*, pp. 94 & 197.

25 Some 67% of Uzbeks felt that nationality relations would get worse in the near future. *Renassans ili regress*, p. 290.

26 *Slovo Kyrgyzstana* 7 January 1992 & 25 February 1992.

27 See the discussion of Russian motivations in various parts of A.I. Ginzburg, et.al, *Russkie v novom zarubezh'e: Kirgiziia* (Moscow, Institute of Ethnology and Anthropology, 1995).

28 For a useful discussion of language politics in Kyrgyzstan see E. Huskey, 'The politics of language in Kyrgyzstan', in *Nationalities Papers*, 23:3 1995, pp. 549–72.

29 *Slovo Kyrgyzstana* 27 January 1995.

30 Under the new proposals put forward by the president in 1997 there would be quotas for women, ethnic minorities and political parties. During a visit to Kyrgyzstan in August/September 1997 I found considerable disagreements over the utility of quotas, with some arguing that the whole idea was pointless, whilst others favoured them for specific groups. Hence the leader of one women's organisation suggested that they were pointless because existing patronage networks would simply ensure the selection of 'their' women, whilst other women's groups saw quotas as the only way of preserving a female presence in the legislature. Similarly, on political parties some argued that given these were largely fictitious why should they have any special rights, whilst one journalist argued that this was the only way to ensure the survival and development of parties.

31 According to K. Karabekov, deputy political editor of Vechernii Bishkek only his paper and *Delo No* were genuinely financially independent, and even they were sometimes cautious about publishing overly critical material. In the case of his own paper he noted that normally such material was subject to a vote by the nine members of the board to determine whether it should be published. Interview with the author, 8 September 1997.

32 Some credence was given to this view by the fact that the old Soviet commissioner for religious affairs had been retained as an adviser by the new state commission, as I discovered during a visit in September 1997.

33 In interviews with Kaptagaev and Deputy Justice Minister Cholponkul Arabaev I was told that the whole affair stemmed from the improper nature of the 1993 gathering and the need for a proper legal constitution of the muftiate. But Kaptagaev also outlined various divisions within the Muslim community, whilst other sources, both printed and private, suggested that the authorities wanted to remove a mufti deemed to be too sympathetic to more radical forms of Islam. I was also told that the whole affair was going to be discussed in a television broadcast which amongst other things claimed that the candidate eventually chosen was not the one favoured by Kaptagaev, but that the programme was taken off the air at the last minute. See the official account of these events published in *Nasha gazeta* 27 May 1997.

34 At a meeting with Muslim leaders in November 1997 he recognised their concerns but warned that religious differences had to be resolved through discussion and persuasion. *Nasha gazeta* 26 November 1997.

35 One of numerous movements created to defend the welfare of the people which failed to survive after their political creators lost interest or, in this case, were arrested.

36 Whilst some in Bishkek describe Akaev as a good man but naive politician, others—including, not surprisingly, the editorial team at *Res publika*—felt that he had learnt on the job and become extremely good at taking the credit where things went well but shifting the blame sideways for less successful or unpopular ventures. Interview with Bermet Bukasheva and Ida Kondrat'eva, 4 September 1997.

37 *Vechernii Bishkek* 13 August 1997.

38 *Nasha gazeta* 20.12.1997.

39 The first quote comes from P. Kasybayev, *Epos Manas* (found at http://www.bishkek.su/krg/Manas-1.html); the second from the same Bishkek cab driver as was quoted regarding corruption.

Chapter 3

THE SWITZERLAND OF THE EAST:
ECONOMIC REFORM IN KYRGYZSTAN

At the end of 1991 the five Central Asian states had only reluctantly accepted their new independent status, all too aware that economically they were extremely dependent upon other Soviet states and that serious restructuring was likely to be socially painful and politically dangerous. Some pinned their hopes on natural resources as a means of underpinning change: Kazakhstan possessed huge oil reserves; Uzbekistan a large reservoir of cheap labour available to would be investors; and in Turkmenistan there was a leader with a vastly inflated sense of his own talents, who saw the exploitation of massive natural gas reserves as capable of turning his country into a new Kuwait. For tiny and mountainous Kyrgyzstan the model to emulate was sometimes seen as Switzerland. Though relatively short of resource potential—leaving aside gold, water and great natural beauty—it was hoped that a rapid adoption of market reforms, the welcoming of foreign investors with open arms, and the creation of a law governed state would give the country a pivotal role in a region wary of market reform. During the early months of his period in office President Askar Akaev committed himself to the creation of a market based economy, and following independence Kyrgyzstan was the first regional state to make serious efforts at putting this commitment into practice. Yet seven years on the picture is more ambiguous, with the country having achieved some success in macro-economic stabilisation, but struggling to extend the benefits of this to the mass of the population. Whilst some have done well out of the changes, over half of the population struggle to make ends meet. In addition the capitalist experiment has brought with it both the technical difficulties that arise in trying to impose Western models of development on a state with very little tradition of capitalism or free market economics, and corruption and criminality on a hitherto unseen scale.

THE INHERITANCE

In seeking to create a new and vital economic system Kyrgyzstan was hampered by the legacy of the past. During the Soviet period the country had been seen by central planners as part of a larger economic unit that included Turkmenistan, Tajikistan, Uzbekistan and the southern regions of Kazakhstan. As part of Moscow's favoured policy of regional specialisation Central Asia had been developed primarily as a producer of raw materials, in particular agricultural products. In the case of Turkmenistan and Uzbekistan the primary crop had been cotton, but in Kyrgyzstan the planners at least took some account of traditional practices in favouring the development of livestock herds. Though herds had been decimated in consequence of the 1916 rebellion and then collectivisation, at the end of the 1980s cattleherding and animal husbandry remained key components of an agricultural sector that continued to employ nearly 40% of the population and account for around one third of Kyrgyz Gross Domestic Product. Inevitably the concentration on livestock brought with it the development of associated products—fodder crops, wool and leather—but the farmers of Kyrgyzstan also produced cereals, sugar beet, tobacco, silk, cotton, some fruit and vegetables. There were also considerable amounts of wild cannabis and opium poppies grown in more remote regions, leading to some rather desultory discussion in the early 1990s of the possibility of legalising the development of this sector. To some extent the choice of agricultural activity was rooted in a regional and ethnic division of labour with cattle especially important in the northern and eastern regions of the country where nomadism had traditionally prevailed, and settled forms of agriculture and products such as fruit and vegetables associated with the Uzbeks of the southern Fergana valley. And whilst the majority of rural production was formally located within the context of state and collective farms, the private sector played a far more important role in this and other Central Asian republics than elsewhere in the USSR. Thus during the 1970s private plots were responsible for the production of 57% of potatoes, 50% of vegetables and 28% of meat. Simultaneously, product value in the years 1970–82 rose by only 11% in the state sector but 67% in the private sphere.[1]

By way of contrast the industrial sector was a latecomer to the Kyrgyz scene, with one Soviet writer pointing out that on the eve of the 1917 revolution only 1,500 people were employed in industry and that most enterprises were devoted to the processing of agricultural goods. Though there was some industrial development during the inter-war years, it was the Great Patriotic War which provided the main impetus to the growth of this sector. During the war numerous factories were transplanted wholesale to Central Asia, often accompanied by Slavic and European workers with the requisite skills and experience. Amongst these were to be found substantial numbers of Germans deported following the Nazi attack on the USSR. During the years following the war the industrial sector mainly located in the northern regions of the country became increasingly diversified, encompassing engineering, the defence sector, the processing of raw materials produced elsewhere, and some exploitation of natural resources. Under the first two categories could be found the production of cars and agricultural equipment, machine tools, electrical equipment from light bulbs to computers, and components for the defence industry—which also used the vast expanse of Lake Issyk Kul to test the Soviet navy's torpedoes. In terms of raw materials Kyrgyzstan lacked the gas and oil potential of some of its neighbours but possessed reserves of various minerals, including coal—producing 43% of the output of the four southern republics—mercury, uranium, zinc, lead and gold, though the potential of the latter was not be fully realised until after independence. Perhaps most important, however, was the country's hydroelectric potential with this largely mountainous and water rich county providing power to a number of neighbouring states during the Soviet era and capable of further development in the future. Finally, Kyrgyzstan under Moscow's rule was involved in the processing of materials produced within the republic and elsewhere, including furniture, textiles, footwear and large amounts of sugar shipped in from Cuba.

Despite this potential the Kyrgyz republic remained amongst the poorest of the Soviet regions, with a GNP per capita of $1,550 in 1991 (compared with $1,350 in Uzbekistan and $2,470 in Kazakhstan). It was also on the eve of independence a republic with growing problems. With a stagnating economy and dynamic population growth—which had doubled the rural population since the 1960s—the republic's inhabitants were facing high levels of underemployment and effective unemployment in rural areas. Moreover, these were issues whose scope extended beyond the narrowly economic, for there was a perception that not only were young Kyrgyz males disportionally affected by the economic down-turn, but that their economic impoverishment and the sheer boredom of unemployment was likely to drive many into anti-social activity, from heavy drinking, through crime to stirring up ethnic hatred. This fear was fuelled by the events of 1990 in the Osh region, where unemployed young males played a key role in the violence, and by the appearance in the cities of large numbers of such people during the early 1990s who simply added further social problems to an infrastructure that could not meet existing needs.

As the country moved towards independence many of these problems were further complicated by the dependent nature of Kyrgyzstan's relationship with other states of the USSR. Figures vary but it appears that in 1991 transfers from the union budget accounted for something like 12% of GDP, though in reality the figure was probably much higher given the central role of all-union enterprises—that is firms essentially subordinate to central agencies in Moscow. In addition the vast majority of Kyrgyzstan's trade, some 98%, was with the countries of the union, with over 40% of imports coming from Russia. Dependence was also evident in other areas, notably the energy sector, with the republic highly dependent upon Uzbekistan for gas and oil. None of this was helped by changing policies in Moscow, and even before Gorbachev started to stress republican self-sufficiency the level of central capital investment in Kyrgyzstan had effectively ceased to grow and the republic received less than any other Central Asian republic. All of these problems were further exacerbated by Soviet collapse which very quickly led to breakdowns in inter-republican trade, the growth of trade barriers between some of these countries, and the withdrawal of financial support from the centre, most notable in the ending of transfers from the union budget and the removal or reduction of subsidies for energy and other products. It was in this context that Kyrgzystan, with very little experience of trade and seemingly little to offer the outside world—earning from exports in 1991 had been lower than that of any other Soviet republic at only $23 million— was thrust into the world economy to fend for itself.

In such circumstances Kyrgyzstan had to tackle the two major tasks facing all the successor states. According to Richard Pomfret, these entail on the one hand negotiating the process of transition and successfully managing the traumatic shift from a centrally planned economy to one in which the market is the dominant force, and on the other promoting development in the broadest sense of the word so as to ensure that any quantitative improvement in the economy raises the living standards and well being of the population as a whole.[2] All this was rendered problematic by the situation which Kyrgyzstan inherited and the task it faced, where economic decline and the needs of political reconstruction complicated further the process of economic reform. Few officials in Kyrgyzstan had any experience of dealing with economic decision making, banking or financial management; few enterprise directors knew how to handle competition or live in a world of hard budget constraints; few workers wanted to live with the threat of unemployment or the jargon of rationalisation and downsizing that came with the new economics; and many skilled Slavic or European professionals felt themselves unwanted and thus left the country rather than contribute their much needed experience to its future development. All of this was to ensure a rough ride for the president and government of the republic as they sought to push through an economic reform of whose value many remained unconvinced.

THE MARKET COMMITMENT

Following his selection as president in October 1990 and more forcefully from the end of 1991, Askar Akaev repeatedly stressed the need for his country to opt for market led reforms. Given the size and limited resource base of his tiny republic such a turn was essential if foreign investors were to be drawn into the process of revitalising the economy and raising the living standards of the population. Moves in this direction began in 1991 when Kyrgyzstan saw the freeing of some prices, and this was taken much further in January 1992 when, following the Russian example, price controls were removed from all but a handful of goods. Where subsidies were retained it was on goods deemed essential to preserve the living standards of the broad mass of the population, and thus some controls remained on domestic fuel, rent, social services, children's food, milk and bread. At the same time the government retained some influence in determining the prices of goods purchased by the state or produced by 'monopolistic enterprises', ie., those with over 35% of domestic market share.[3] In 1993 in the face of growing economic crisis the government appears to have intervened further to control prices, but from 1994 gradually withdrew from this area with the majority of prices finally freed from state controls, with bread subsidies gradually phased out and the support for energy prices reduced if not fully eliminated. Alongside price liberalisation went the development of an austerity programme which Akaev persuaded a reluctant parliament to accept and the development of the first phase of a privatisation programme which aimed to remove about a third of enterprises from state control by the end of 1993.

Such moves towards the market did not go unchallenged, and a number of political commentators were critical of the mad dash to the market and what they saw as a tendency to throw out the baby with the bathwater in the economic sector. Perhaps not surprisingly the Communist Party was at the forefront of criticism, sometimes using nationalistic arguments to support its critique. In February 1993 in an appeal to the political elite the party attacked the fact that economic policy was being determined by the IMF and foreign investors in a way which undermined Kyrgyz sovereignty. Though recognising the need for some degree of marketisation, they stressed the need for a 'regulated market' which balanced the needs of reform with the social well being of the population. Several months later Communist Party leader Jumgalbek Amanbaev added a more pragmatic argument, suggesting that in areas where the old economic system delivered the goods it would be better not to change. In the agricultural sphere this might entail hanging on to the old collective forms of organisation, and in support of this he claimed that collective enterprise had created the conditions in which livestock herds had been built up since the 1920s. At the same time Amanbaev quoted various figures suggesting that public farming in Kyrgyzstan had been more productive than private farming in Iran and Turkey during the 1980s, statistics he used to re-emphasise his party's opposition to any move towards private land ownership. Criticism of marketisation also came from the trade unions, who noted the social effects of reform and its deleterious effects on large sections of the population—with the chairman of the main union federation claiming in early 1993 that 98% were below the official poverty level. Though such a figure overstated the real position, there could be little doubt that economic change was leading to serious problems for substantial sections of the population. In such circumstances it was perhaps not surprising to find many contributors to the constitutional debates of 1992–93 calling for much stronger guarantees of the right to work and to social welfare. For example, the chairman of the Council of the Federation of Trade Unions of Kyrgyzstan attacked the constitutional draft for its vague formulation of socio-economic rights and suggested a simple restoration of the clauses of the Soviet era constitution which offered much firmer guarantees of the right to work and welfare.[4]

A major problem facing the republic in the early stages of reform was the acceleration of inflation levels, jumping from around 200% in 1991 to over 900% in 1992. For Kyrgyzstan the problem was exacerbated further by its participation in the rouble zone, growing pressures stemming from Russian monetary policy and involvement in a situation where most of the former Soviet states continued to use the rouble but each developed their own credit and monetary policies. Seeking to escape the high inflation rates of the Commonwealth of Independent States, settle its debts with Russia, reduce its dependence upon Moscow, and attract foreign investors Kyrgystan took the decision to introduce its own currency, the som, in May 1993. Not all were convinced. Though parliament voted 211–41 in favour, many deputies expressed unhappiness about what they saw as an over-hasty introduction of the new currency. Some claimed that they had been given too little information and asked whether the country's economy was sufficiently stabilised to support a new currency. Others asked why Akaev had shifted from his earlier opposition to this measure, to which the president responded with the politician's classic defence by referring to changing circumstances—in this case created by Russian monetary and trade policies. Other deputies expressed concern over how the change might affect Kyrgyzstan's neighbours and in particular the trading relations of the residents of Osh and Jalalabad with Uzbekistan. Such fears were not unfounded, for the introduction of the som and the limited consultation with surrounding states prior to its introduction were to cause frictions, more easily papered over with Kazakhstan, but more damaging with Uzbekistan. Almost immediately the latter's president Islam Karimov decreed the cessation of energy links with Kyrgyzstan and required travellers and traders coming from the republic to use dollars. There were also problems in economic relations with other CIS states, as suppliers in Russia and elsewhere refused to accept payment in som and thus forced local enterprises to lay off workers and limit their activities. Yet though the introduction of the som had perhaps been insufficiently prepared, with the backing of a $62 million credit from the IMF the currency found its feet and contributed to long-term macro-economic stabilisation. Relations with Uzbekistan remained frosty for a while, but in June 1993 a series of economic accords between Tashkent and Bishkek, which included a formal commitment to use the dollar as the basis of inter-bank exchange, restored relations and in any case, within six months both Kazakhstan and Uzbekistan were forced by Russian demands to cut loose from the rouble zone and create their own currencies.[5]

As noted earlier, a key plank of Kyrgyzstan's reform programme has been privatisation, the first stage of which aimed at selling off around one third of state enterprises and two thirds of housing stock within two years. This was to be achieved by various means, including selling to individuals, collective buyouts by management and workers, or the creation of joint stock companies in which some shares would be sold to those involved in the enterprise and others distributed to the public in a voucher scheme. Those sectors targetted by the increasingly important State Property Fund were to include services, trade, and catering in the first instance followed later by larger industrial concerns which employed far more people and whose subsequent success or failure would thus have a far greater impact upon economic development. At the same time it was made clear that during this initial period certain sectors were off limits, including those concerned with transport, utilities, defence and mineral resources. In early 1994 the process was taken further as coupons were distributed to every citizen allowing them to buy shares in various types of enterprise and, despite an initial lack of interest, by mid-1996 the World Bank could report that over 60% of these had been invested. Alongside the voucher schemes went various other approaches designed to draw managers and employees into participating in the development of their own industries, as well as relatively unsuccessful efforts to draw in foreign investors—who from late 1995 were able to own 100% of companies as opposed to the previous 49%.

By mid-1996 over 900 medium and large scale enterprises had been more or less privatised (the state retained an interest in some), and by mid-1997 some 61% of formerly state owned enterprises had been taken over by the private sector. In addition plans were being drawn up to sell off major state companies in the transport and energy sector, though the latter proposals were drawing considerable criticism in mid-1997 from sections of the media and some deputies. Despite enjoying some success in removing enterprises from the state sector, the privatisation process has not been unproblematic in a country with very little experience or even real understanding of market economics. In the early stages changes of ownership brought little alteration in enterprise behaviour as the government imposed no hard budget constraints and employee shareholders understandably exhibited little real enthusiasm for any restructuring that might reduce the size of the workforce. In most cases the existing managements remained in place, people who as a rule exhibited little entrepreneurial spirit. And for those that remained in the state or quasi-state sector there was even less incentive to change as the state remained unwilling to let industries fail. Despite the enactment of a bankruptcy law in 1996 only 29 firms had been cut off from bank credit by the end of that year and were then subject to liquidation or substantial restructuring prior to privatisation.[6]

Alongside these practical issues went political concerns about whether private ownership was of necessity preferable to that of the state. Critics pointed out that privatisation might concentrate power in the hands of the old nomenklatura class and particular clan groups within the republic, or that it would allow national assets to be taken over by foreign investors who were not primarily concerned with the republic's well being. Some of these problems were discussed in a confidential report on the privatisation process produced by Interior Minister Feliks Kulov in the spring of 1997 which pointed to some of the quasi-criminal activities taking place in this area. In particular there was a feeling that many state enterprises were being sold off at unjustifiably low prices and that finance companies were buying up coupons relatively cheaply from ordinary citizens and using them to make huge profits. Following this report and the publicity over the case of an Osh silk factory valued at 93 million som and sold for less than 2 million, Akaev issued a decree in May 1997 which called a temporary halt to further privatisations except those achieved by auction.[7]

The creation of a Kyrgyz currency and the extension of privatisation has required the establishment of an appropriate banking and financial sector, as well as the organisation of a forum where companies can attract investment for their future development. Following independence, a National Bank of Kyrgyzstan was formed, with broad responsibility for the development or monetary and exchange rate policy, as well as for the oversight of the wider banking sector. Though initially depicted as responsible to parliament, in practice the 1996 constitutional amendments which gave the oversight of economic policy to the president have meant that Akaev plays an active role in overseeing the work of this institution potentially central to the success of economic reform. According to some outside experts the bank, and its current young chairman Marat Sultanov, have proved especially receptive to taking on board the lessons of international practice. And since the collapse and liquidation of several banks in the first half of the 1990s, the National Bank has sought to evolve a greater regulatory capacity to ensure domestic and international confidence in the banking system. Hence in January 1997 nine of the major banks, in consultation with the central bank, adopted international accounting standards.

The development of a stock exchange has been more problematic, as many Kyrgyz businessmen had little understanding of the role played by capital and security markets, and in 1997 the Kyrgyz parliament was still considering a law providing proper regulation of the activities of the securities market. American observers commenting on this have noted the tendency of many Kyrgyz with capital to invest to opt for cars or other depreciating assets, rather than Kyrgyz industry. They also suggested that though upwards of 400 companies may have the capacity to enter the market, less than 70 had actually registered with the Kyrgyz stock exchange by the end of 1997. Yet the potential advantages of doing so were immense, as extra capital generated through the market might lead to the employment of more workers which would then increase spending power in the economy. Though the National Bank chairman described the Kyrgyz economy as steering along the top of a gulf, it did appear that by 1997 some degree of stability and continuity were emerging in the financial and banking sector in Kyrgyzstan.[8] If parliament and president could push through further laws for the regulation of the market, and survive the threats posed by corruption, then this sector might acquire domestic and international confidence, and *might* in turn contribute to the furtherance of economic recovery and growth.

AGRICULTURE AND LAND REFORM

In a country where a substantial section of the population still lives and works in the rural sector, the agricultural question remains a vital one. Since the late 1980s if not earlier, the rural sector has been in crisis as an increasingly inefficient agricultural sector failed to provide sufficient employment for a growing population. With the collapse of the Soviet system the problem initially worsened, with a substantial fall in output recorded during the first few years of independence. Though statistics are not entirely reliable, the International Monetary Fund reported agricultural output declining by 9% in 1991,19% in 1992, 10% in 1993 and 15% in 1994. Especially disastrous has been the reported decline in livestock herds which some sources claim fell by substantial amounts during the early 1990s (see table 3). During the winter of 1992–93 the position was made worse by the fact that in the face of economic decline and fodder shortages, as well as the loss of export markets in Russian, many farmers slaughtered their cattle. Though some commentators suggested that the figures were not as bad as reported because many private farmers misreported the number of animals in their possession in order to avoid taxation and control, in September 1997 the agriculture ministry was warning that meat shortages were imminent. This problem was given further credence by newspaper reports of a growth in cattle rustling—a trend brought home to the author on a journey between the Chu and Naryn region during the summer of 1997 when the car he was travelling in was stopped twice by the militia looking not, as he had assumed, for drugs but for stolen animals.[9]

Table 3:   Reduction in head of cattle and birds, in thousands

	Large cattle	Including cows	Pigs*	Sheep and goats	Horses	Birds
1993	1122,4	514,7	246,6	8741,5	313,0	10420,5
1994	1062,3	511,2	169,4	7322,3	322,0	6916,5
1995	920,1	480,9	117,8	5076,4	299,0	2208,5
1996	869,0	470,9	113,9	4274,8	308,1	2031,8
1997	847,6	459,9	88,1	3716,1	314,1	2122,4

* One might speculate that the dramatic reduction in the number of pigs stemmed from a rediscovery of the country's Islamic traditions, however attentuated in practice these may be.
Source: *Kyrgyzstan v tsifrakh, 1996,* Bishkek, National Statistical Committee of the Kyrgyz Republic, 1997, p. 194

More recently there have been some signs of improvement for those farmers with access to funds for modernisation and restructuring, with help from international agencies such as the Asian Development Bank, the World Bank, and the European Bank for Reconstruction and Development which has offered support for projects centred on the better management of livestock pastures, the rehabilitation of irrigation networks and the provision of machinery, seed and fertilisers. Such efforts appeared to be bearing fruit with much improved grain harvests in 1996 and 1997, enabling the country to meet the needs of the domestic market and leaving some for export. At the same time it was reported that 1996 witnessed the first rise in agricultural production since the achievement of independence. Nonetheless, the countryside offers a mixed picture of success story and tragedy, with some private farmers doing very well in the new system—often a classic outworking of the biblical principle that to those who have will more be given—but many ordinary village dwellers falling into poverty. None of this has been helped by continued population growth (albeit showing some signs of slowing down) in the villages which leaves many young people effectively unemployed or with only the opportunity for seasonal employment.

Throughout the period developments in the countryside have been the subject of considerable political controversy, with allegations of corruption levelled at agriculture ministers and official peasant organisations, and fierce disputes as to the best way forward for the rural sector.[10] Nowhere have the debates been more acerbic than on the troubled question of land ownership. From 1991 President Akaev persistently argued that the best means of stimulating the agricultural sector would be to admit the principle of private land ownership. In early 1994 a presidential decree gave individuals or legal entities the right to lease and cultivate plots of land for 49 years and allowed for the exchange or sale of leases, but only to other Kyrgyz citizens. In November 1995 this was extended to 99 years, whilst during his presidential campaign at the end of that year Akaev made clear his intention to push for private land ownership in the future. Simultaneously he encouraged the distribution of land use shares in agricultural land which effectively led to the break up of most state and collective farms and their replacement by agricultural cooperatives. To many Kyrgyz commentators the notion of private landownership was anathema, with the Communists hostile to the very idea of privatising the land and nationalists suggesting that the principle was alien to Kyrgyz traditions and expressing fears that the best land would be bought up by Russians, Uzbeks or other foreigners. For the traditionalists, land was something that belonged to all those living on its territory which could be privately used but had to be publicly owned. Hence the leasing system was acceptable but private ownership was not. Such a tradition might not be unchangeable but critics argued that it could not be over-turned rapidly or by presidential decree. Akaev, however, remained unconvinced and continued to push for change. In late 1996 he issued a decree effectively permitting private landownership from the beginning of 1997.

INTERNATIONAL INVOLVEMENT IN ECONOMIC DEVELOPMENT

In pushing hard for rapid marketisation from the outset, Akaev was motivated in part by a realisation of Kyrgyzstan's limited resource potential and its inaccessibility, and thus took the view that only by adopting such a pro-reform position in advance of many neighbouring states could his country hope to attract investment and economic support from the outside world. The pursuit of this goal entailed a number of strategies, including: approaching international financial institutions to provide help for stabilisation policies; looking for foreign investment in restructuring sectors such as transport, communications and energy that would underlie any successful restructuring; and seeking investment in the development of areas such as gold extraction where the republic had considerable potential. In the first of these Akaev enjoyed considerable success, with the IMF providing over $60 million to back up the introduction of the som in May 1993, and the World Bank offering a number of substantial credits to support various aspects of the reform programme. These included providing financial and technical know-how for the privatisation programme, backing for the restructuring of the financial sector, limited allocation of support for state welfare provision and, in the spring of 1997, some $44 million to help reduce the budget deficit. Other financial institutions have also played a role here, with the European Bank for Reconstruction and Development (EBRD) and the Asian Development Bank (ADB) especially prominent. The former has so far offered over $100 million to support the upgrading of telecommunications, small and medium size businesses, the development of the Kumtor gold mine, the restructuring of the electricity network in the Issyk Kul region and the creation of agro-business firms to help farmers develop new techniques and improve their efficiency. Even larger amounts of credit have been provided by the ADB, with their financial support concentrated on agricultural reform and modernisation of the Bishkek-Osh highway.

Whilst Kyrgyzstan has generated considerable international financial support for economic restructuring, its record in encouraging direct investment has been mixed. Though on paper entry into the Kyrgyz market is far simpler than in many CIS states, would be investors still have to jump various bureaucratic hurdles, operate within an only partially worked out legal framework, and decide how to tackle the corruption that pervades economic relationships throughout the region. To facilitate foreign investment government and parliament have simplified procedures for international involvement in economic life, passed a series of laws regulating foreign businesses, and made it possible for them to acquire majority holdings in Kyrgyz businesses. In addition it has offered substantial tax breaks, especially to those who reinvest significant portions of their profits within Kyrgyzstan. Free economic zones (FEZ) have been created, notably in the Naryn oblast which has primarily attracted Chinese investors, in Karakol, and then from 1996 the Bishkek FEZ encompassing the international airport and surrounding area.[11] Though many foreign companies remain wary of investing in an area about which they know little and whose stability remains in doubt, a growing number of foreign investors have been encouraged by the government's efforts to ease their way, evident in the creation of an Agency for Direct Foreign Investment in April 1996 and the passage of the first part of the Civil Code which came into operation several months later and effectively promised equal rights to foreign and domestic companies.

Thoughout this period the single largest investment project has been that connected with the development of the Kumtor gold field, a joint project involving the state gold company Kyrgyzaltyn and Canada's Cameco corporation. With gold reserves estimated at over 500 metric tons and valued at $6,500m the Kumtor field was always going to be attractive to foreign investors, and the joint project quickly gained financial backing from the EBRD, Canada's Export and Development Coorporation, and the Chase Manhattan Bank. This allowed some $375m. to be devoted to the development of this mountainous and relatively inaccessible site which the Soviet authorities had investigated but deemed too expensive to develop. From the beginning the project faced considerable difficulties as a separate gold scandal made many suspicious of the way in which contracts were awarded and the government sought to ensure that Kyrgyzstan got a good deal out the project. Further problems stemmed from the site itself, located at around 4000 metres, reached by poor roads, and offering little in the way of comfort or infrastructure for those who worked there. In addition, development has been dogged by a series of accidents which have cost both foreign and local lives. Nonetheless, by the mid-1990s a deal had been done which gave the Kyrgyz over 70% of the profits and by 1997 the open cast mining phase had begun to produce, with over 4 tons of gold mined during the first five months of that year. During the first nine months of 1997 alone the developing gold industry created nearly 800 new jobs in the republic.

As a result of this project Canada accounts for the vast majority of direct investment in the republic, and the Issyk Kul region remains the major recipient. Other major investors included Turkey—which has been involved in construction and catering—Switzerland, the USA, Russia, Italy, Germany and Ireland, though if one broadens this out to include trade relations China—much of whose trading with Kyrgyzstan goes unrecorded—and other CIS countries also remain major players. From the early 1990s numerous foreign companies were granted licenses to produce their goods in Kyrgyzstan, with the major cola rivals amongst the more obvious of these in recent years. During the years 1993–95 the republic received around $720m in credits and $150m in technical help. Of this 29.7% came from the World

Bank, 13.1% from the IMF, 14.5% from Japan—which amongst other things is playing a key role in financing the modernisation of Bishkek's Manas airport—11% from the Asian Development Bank, 10.4% from Turkey and 7% from Switzerland, Germany and Denmark. And of this 39.5% was devoted to macro-economic stabilisation, 29.5% to the development of production, 13.5% to imports and 16.8% to creating a minimum social safety net.[12] There were also some signs that Kyrgyzstan's formal commitment to democratisation had paid off, evident in the fact that during the mid-1990s the United States Agency for International Development (USAID) was providing 16 times as much per head to Kyrgyzstan as it was to Uzbekistan.[13]

Whilst discussion of foreign involvement tends to focus on relations with the industrialised world, in practice the majority of Kyrgyzstan's economic connections remain with the former Soviet Union, with nearly 80% of its exports heading towards the CIS and around 60% of its imports coming from former Soviet countries. The importance of ties within the CIS has been clearly recognised by the authorities in Bishkek, and has disposed Kyrgyzstan to enter various unions within the former Soviet space. Of these the most important were the economic union developed with Kazakhstan and Uzbekistan in 1994 which was intended to create a common economic space by the end of the century, and the decision to join a customs union with Russia, Belarus and Kazakhstan in March 1996 which aims to establish a single market along European Union lines. In addition there has been some desultory talk of the possibility of an economic union between Kazakhstan and Kyrgyzstan which would give formal recognition to a considerable degree of de facto integration. Yet the latter proposal appears to have fallen by the wayside in 1997 as tensions mounted between the countries over issues such as water supplies and the taxation of goods crossing Kazakh borders. Equally, there are serious questions being raised about membership in the first two unions, with their substance and the compatibility of membership in both questioned by some.

Nonetheless, Kyrgyzstan's participation in these organisations indicates a clear recognition that the close ties built up over decades cannot be removed overnight. At the same time this involvement stems from a perception of a natural affinity of interest between these states based upon both their geographical position and historical experience. For all this, relations between these states have not always been easy. Bishkek's hasty introduction of the som created tensions with Kazakhstan and Uzbekistan, and reinforced the latter's suspicion of Kyrgyzstan's relatively liberal polity. Tensions have also arisen over energy and natural resources, with Kyrgyzstan highly dependent upon Uzbekistan for supplies of natural gas and on more than one occasion seeing Tashkent cut of its supplies when Bishkek got behind in its payments. Equally, the decision of the Kyrgyz parliament in mid-1997 to charge Tashkent for water originating in Kyrgyz reservoirs may do little for relations between these two countries. Relations with Russia have generally been more amicable, though the level of debt has forced Kyrgyzstan to hand over a considerable stake in a number of local companies to Russian state or private investors. Thus in early 1996 Russian companies took majority share holdings in several tobacco firms, a chemical plant, as well as minority holdings in various light industries. A decision was also taken to merge the Kyrgyz hydroelectric companies with their Russian equivalents who took a 49% stake in the Kyrgz state company, on paper a mutually advantageous deal which provides Russia with cheap electricity and Kyrgyzstan with guaranteed exports. Such decisions, whilst inevitably arousing the ire of the more nationalistically minded, point to the fact that for the foreseeable future Kyrgyzstan's primary economic partners are likely to remain the Soviet successor states. More importantly, they remind Kyrgyz politicians that whilst the relationship may be extremely unequal, it is not without benefit for this new state cast adrift in an often harsh economic world; without Russian contracts—such as that acquired by the Dastan company to build Russian planes at the beginning of October 1997—life might be much harder.

PROBLEMS AND PROSPECTS

The first few years of independence saw the Kyrgyz economy in free fall as output fell dramatically and inflation soared. From 1992–95 GDP fell by around 45%, with agricultural production falling by around a third and industrial production by nearly two-thirds. Alongside this went inflation rates of over 900% in 1992 and 1,300% in 1993 and a fiscal budget deficit of 12% in 1992 and 8% in 1994. Though, as internal critics were quick to point out, these problems were far greater than those suffered in neighbouring Uzbekistan, this stemmed in large part from the relative rapidity with which reform was introduced in Kyrgystan compared with some of its neigh-bours.[14] And despite these difficulties there has since 1995 been some evidence of economic stabilisation and indications of future growth, albeit from a relatively low starting point, with reported rises in both industrial and agricultural output.

Yet macro-economic stabilisation remains only part of the picture and disguises continuing economic problems, some of a more technical nature relating to the implementation of market reforms in a country without

Table 4:   Key economic indicators, 1992–6, expressed as a
percentage of the previous year.

	1992	1993	1994	1995	1996
GDP	86.1	84.5	79.9	94.6	105.6
Industrial production	73.6	75.4	72.1	82.2	110.8
Production of consumer goods	66.8	80.4	60.2	74.0	117.7
Agricultural production	94.5	90.2	81.5	98.0	113.1
Capital investments	75.0	77.4	55.4	81.7	106.5

Source: *Kyrgyzstan v tsifrakh, 1996*, Bishkek, National Statistical Committee of the
Kyrgyz Republic, 1997, p. 10.

experience or adequate infrastructure, and some of a more practical nature. The legal and cultural basis for private enterprise remains ambiguous for both domestic and foreign entrepreneurs, and corruption remains endemic. Problems for economic development also stemmed from the very geography of the country and the largely inadequate transport infrastructure linking the various sections of this mountainous land. Most major roads remained in a state of poor repair, the only rail link ran along the north of the country as far as the western shores of Lake Issyk Kul, whilst air connections were hampered at least initially by irregular fuel supplies and doubtful safety standards. This in turn had a knock on effect not only on encouraging investment, but also in developing the considerable tourist potential of a land with great natural beauty which might attract those interested in climbing, skiing or wildlife. Various projects have been initiated to improve connections, with Japanese investment to aid in the modernisation of Bishkek airport, and work already started on the upgrading of the Bishkek-Osh highway whose landslides claim many lives every year. During 1997 plans were also announced to develop a north–south rail link which would eventually connect Kyrgyzstan to the countries of Persian Gulf and Indo-China, but as with the other plans these will all take time to realise and deliver economic benefit to the country.

Further practical difficulties face the state in seeking to ensure that its own workers are paid, problems engendered in part by the difficulties of revenue collection in a context where production levels are hard to assess and even harder to tax, and where over a tenth of production is accounted for by the 'black-economy'. In consequence the government newspaper *Nasha gazeta* could report in May 1997 that tax crimes accounted for around 12% of criminal activities in Kyrgyzstan, and that tax avoidance had become big business.[15] Other reports suggested that economic crime, including the disappearance of substantial amounts of state investment and foreign aid earmarked for agriculture and the development of the gold industry, was costing the state millions of dollars every month and that amongst the worst offenders were businessmen with seats in the country's parliament.[16] Amongst the various ploys developed by rogue businessmen was the creation of phoney joint ventures which then applied for the tax breaks enjoyed by external investors. Such problems had knock-on effects for government credibility, for if the state could not collect revenue it could not pay its workers or provide pensions, and when this happened it was the government or the reform progamme that was blamed not those who failed to pay their taxes.

Cold economic statistics reporting success also did little justice to the real problems faced by substantial sections of the population. Living standards fell dramatically, with real income per head falling by two-thirds, and unemployment rose, with official statistics claiming 140,000 people or 13% of the working age population out of work by the beginning of 1996. Such figures, however, disguised a much larger problem for it excluded those who failed to register and those who had to survive on seasonal employment, and most commentators within the country have suggested that a minimum of 20% of the population was in fact unemployed and that many more were only in work for part of the year. Problems were particularly acute for those in the industrial sector—with many industries closed down or their workforces 'downsized' during the early 1990s—and for those living in the southern regions of Osh and Jalalabad which have been badly hit by economic decline. Further difficulties were posed for many of those in work by the fact that delays in payment left many workers without an income for months on end.

Assessing the full extent of the problem is not easy and clearly some sectors of the population were more affected than others. According to a 1993 World Bank report, 39.7% of households and 45.4% of individuals were classified as poor and over 80% of the population as 'underprovisioned'.[17] Figures produced three years later suggested that 60% of the population lived below the official poverty line and that 18% of the population was in 'extreme poverty'.[18] These figures in turn disguised other divisions, with the bulk of poverty experienced in rural areas and the southern regions of the country. Other evidence also pointed to the problems faced by those on fixed incomes such as pensioners and invalids, single parents or those with large families—especially as the payment of such state benefits as did exist was often months behind schedule. And although more men than women registered as unemployed during the early 1990s, many of the social problems that ensued from the economic decline fell more heavily upon women in their capacity as domestic workers, reproductive agents and child rearers. Numerous reports pointed to the problems facing women in the new environment for, though they had traditionally played a more active public role than in neighbouring states, economic decline and the 'rediscovery' of traditional customs threatened such gains as they had made during the Soviet period. A number of politicians argued that the time had come to restore the traditional dignity of women by taking them out of the workplace, whilst others sought to 'protect' women by encouraging polygamy and supporting the decriminalisation of certain marraige customs forbidden during the Soviet era.[19] And though the state paid lip service to the rights of women, evident in the creation of a commission on women and the family and of an inter-departmental commission to ensure that all ministries and departments thought about the impact of their activities on women, in practice reduced state revenues and expenditure severely limited such actions.[20]

Whilst impoverishment was evident in falling real incomes, other broader factors indicated a general decline in the quality of life of many citizens of Kyrgyzstan. Almost inevitably the new state found it impossible to provide the level of investment in health care and education that was necessary to maintain and improve public well-being, and countless statistics pointed to the problems emerging in this areas. According to some sources the growth in the number of visits to 'holy places' in part stemmed from the collapse of the health system, and official figures showed that nearly 10% of children were chronically hungry.[21] Similar problems affected education, with the ending of almost all state provided pre-school education in 1993, many schools closing from lack of funds and over 20,000 children reportedly not attending school in 1996 owing to lack of winter clothes and the poor availability of transport in rural areas. All of these problems disporportionately affected the rural areas of the country where larger families prevailed, notably the Naryn region where fertility rates were twice that of the two northern regions and the capital, and in Osh and Jalalabad where they were 50% higher.

The breakdown in services affected the most basic supplies, with water provision interrupted in many parts of the south and reports that an increasing number of people were resorting to irrigation ditches for their supplies.[22] Though the state has sought to reform the welfare system in order to focus attention on those in most need, inevitably such a reform takes time to operate properly and is difficult to manage in a situation where such large sections of the population are facing acute problems and public expenditure is limited by harsh economic reality.

In these circumstances families are forced to resort to various defence mechanisms. As outlined by Jude Howell, these include increased borrowing from families and friends—difficult if you were not in a position to recip-rocate—reducing consumption, relying on wild foodstuffs and drawing on reserves—though savings soon run out and livestock killed for food cannot produce milk or reproduce—or learning new trades and skills, notably trad-ing in the new free market context. Here much appears to depend upon the existence of entrepreneurial individuals, groups or associations who can join together to initiate local responses to specific problems.[23] To these responses one should add the resort to criminal activities, with the Kyrgyz trade union organisations blaming much of the growing crime problem and the tempta-tion of involvement in drug trafficking on the economic situation which many find themselves in.

By mid-1997 Kyrgyzstan's economic prospects appeared slightly better than a few years earlier. Its currency was relatively stable and inflation fell to just over 30% in 1996—though 44% for foodstuffs—compared with 77% in Uzbekistan and 60% in Kazakhstan. At the same time there were signs of growth with Gross National Product up by 5.6%, industrial production up by 10.8% and agricultural production reportedly up by 13.1% on the previ-ous year's figures. Moreover, early indications from 1997 suggest similar improvements with the largest production increase in the CIS reported by Kyrgyzstan during the first six months of that year.[24] Yet this was growth from a much reduced base and an improvement whose effect was yet to be felt by the population. Real unemployment was perhaps as high as 20% with young rural males continuing to flock to the capital in search of work, and inequality was more obvious as the few who did well out of the new system flaunted their wealth through flashy cars and new, well guarded homes, and were able to ensure for themselves and their children the education and health care that was increasingly unavailable for many. Small gestures were made to some of these groups, as in Akaev's June 1997 decree assigning 8% of shares in leading companies to pensioners,[25] but these were likely to make little impact upon their daily lives. More importantly, they did little to alleviate the potential for social tensions between urban and rural dwellers, evident in the negative reaction of many Bishkek residents to the appearance of the Yntymak movement which further extended the shanty towns of the capital. All of these issues presented serious difficulties for a president and government struggling to build a new economic system based upon market principles and create public faith in the new Kyrgyzstan as a society and political system concerned for the welfare of all of its citizens.

1 B. Rumer, *Soviet Central Asia—A Tragic Experiment* (London, Unwin Hyman, 1989), pp. 126–7.

2 R. Pomfret, *The Economies of Central Asia* (Princeton, Princeton University Press, 1995), pp. 6–7.

3 I have relied here and elsewhere on the discussion of the early period of economic reform provided in M. Dabrowski, et.al., 'Economic reforms in Kyrgyzstan', in *Communist Economics and Economic Transformation*, 7:3, 1995, pp. 269–97.

4 *Slovo kyrgyzstana* 19 Feburary 1993; similar demands for greater guarantees were made by the leader of the Kyrgyz Women's Committee who feared that in the new atmosphere the rights of women were likely to suffer as the economy declined and traditional customs were revived. *Slovo Kyrgyzstana* 2 April 1993.

5 On currency reform in Kyrgyzstan see Pomfret, *The Economies of Central Asia*, pp. 144–6; E. Huskey, 'Kyrgyzstan leaves the rouble zone', in *RFE/RL Research Report*, 3 September 1994, pp. 38–43; L. Maillet, 'New states initiate new currencies', *Transition*, 9 June 1995, pp. 44–49 & 56.

6 See M. Kaser, 'Economic transition in six Central Asian economies', in *Central Asian Survey*, 16:1, 1997, pp. 18–19; *Kyrgyzstan v tsifrakh 1996* (Bishkek, National Statisticial Committee of the Kyrgyz Republic, 1997), pp. 167–8 provides some information on the various types of privatisation and reports nearly 80% of housing stock as having been sold of by the beginning of 1997.

7 *Nasha gazeta* 23 May 1997.

8 'USAID helps "mobilise" Kyrgyzstan's capital', in *The Central Asian Post*, 6 November 1997.

9 There were a reported 670 cases in the Naryn region during the first eight months of 1997. *Vechernii Bishkek* 25 September 1997.

10 See the discussion in *Central Asian Post* 29 May 1997.

11 During conversations in the Naryn oblast it was suggested that the Naryn FEZ was so far largely a paper organisation rather than a genuine stimulus for investment.

12 *Res publika* 5 June 1996.

13 *Slovo Kyrgyzstana* 24 May 1995.

14 Pomfret, *The Economies of Central Asia*, p. 47.

15 *Nasha Gazeta* 2 May 1997.

16 In November 1997 the capital's evening paper listed 173 deputies at all levels, including ten in the national parliament, who had been involved in criminal activities. *Vechernii Bishkek* 7 November 1997.

17 Jude Howell, 'Poverty and transition in Kyrgyzstan: how some households cope', in *Central Asian Survey*, 15: 1, 1996, pp. 60–1.

18 *Kyrgyzstan Analysis Report: Living Standards and Measurement Survey* (Bishkek, National Statistical Committee of the Kyrgyz Republic and Research Triangle Institute, 1997), pp. 7 & 10.

19 The problems faced by women were especially acute, as their selection as the first 'victims' of reform contrasted sharply with their relatively (compared to other central Asian states) extensive involvement in economic and public life. Moreover, it was exacerbated by the revival of traditional customs which many saw as providing a justification for returning women to their domestic roles. See the two useful books produced by the Bishkek based women's organisation Diamond: *Zhenshchiny kyrgyzstana: traditsii i novaia realnost'* (Bishkek, 1995) and *Nenadezhnost' gendernoi zashchity* (Bishkek, 1996), and the statistical report on the position of women sponsored by the United Nations Development Project: *Women of the Kyrgyz Republic* (Bishkek, National Statistical Committee of the Kyrgyz Republic, 1997).

20 Interview with Jamal Tashibekova, chairperson of the state commission on women, young people and the family, 9 September 1997. She reported that so far her commission had received only about a third of the money allocated in the budget, though stressed that this indicated less the government's lack of commitment to the task than the general economic crisis.

21 *Vechernii Bishkek* 14 August 1997.

22 I am grateful to Medetbek Sultanbaev for providing me with this information, some of which can be found in *Atazhurt* 25–30 October 1996.

23 Jude Howell, 'Coping with transition: insights from Kyrgyzstan', in *Third World Quarterly*, 17:1, 1996, pp. 53–68, and 'Poverty and transition in Kyrgyzstan', pp. 59–73.

24 *Nasha gazeta* 25 July 1997.

25 Radio Free Europe/Radio Liberty, *Daily Report*, 10 June 1997.

Chapter 4

KYRGYZ SECURITY IN A POST-SOVIET ERA

Sometimes it seems as if small states are like small boats, pushed out into a turbulent sea, free in one sense to traverse it; but, without oars or provisions, without compass or sails, free also to perish. Or, perhaps, to be rescued and taken on board a larger vessel.[1]

These comments by former Secretary-General of the British Commonwealth, Shridath Ramphal, might have been designed for states such as Kyrgyzstan; somewhat reluctantly cast adrift by a USSR that was breaking up, and not quite sure how to survive in a dangerous world. In this new situation the successor states that emerged out of the Soviet Union had to work out their own perception of the national interest, to isolate potential challenges to their security and stability, and to develop mechanisms for coping with their new found status as independent actors on the world stage. In this chapter I explore some of the foreign policy and security issues facing Kyrgyzstan, and start by examining the mechanisms and institutions which have been created to meet the challenges of the 1990s. In particular I point to the key role of the president in directing foreign policy, the role of the foreign ministry and the military, and the much broader definition of security evident in the role assigned to the state Security Council formed in early 1994. This broader understanding is discussed in the second section which isolates the challenges to the new state posed by ethnic conflict, religious extremism, criminality and the drug trade, and the difficulties stemming from persistent conflict in neighbouring Tajikistan. All of these problems threatened to undermine Kyrgyz efforts to establish civic peace within the republic, something that was essential if the new state was to rebuild the political and economic order. In the third section we very briefly point to the development of relations with the outside world, where the desire to find new partners has gone hand in hand with a recognition that the old ties built up over a century or more cannot easily be undone. Hence Kyrgyzstan has sought closer economic relations with the West, the Middle East and with Asia, whilst remaining sensitive to the concerns of would be regional superpowers such as Russia, Uzbekistan, Kazkhstan and China.[2]

FOREIGN POLICY AND SECURITY INSTITUTIONS

During the Soviet era foreign policy making had largely been handled from Moscow and few Central Asians were given experience at high levels within the foreign ministry. Under Gorbachev the writer Chingiz Aitmatov had served as ambassador to Luxembourg and Roza Otunbaeva, with some experience in the Soviet foreign service as head of the ministry's UNESCO commission, was appointed ambassador to Malaysia. Such people were rare however, and within the republic there were few people who had been seriously involved in international politics or the potentially more important area of foreign trade. At the same time, when the USSR collapsed Kyrgyzstan lacked the financial resources to open diplomatic representations in more than a few countries. For that reason it had to rely on the good offices of Russia, other CIS countries and Turkey to represent its interests abroad.

Though the 1993 constitution gave parliament the right to determine the general direction of foreign policy, most recognised that in practice President Akaev would play a key role, in particular in seeking to balance the need to maintain good relations with Russia and the search for foreign partners to aid in the rebuilding process. At the same time there was some discussion during the early 1990s of the possibility of 'peoples' diplomacy', with a somewhat visionary hope that in the new order there might be some scope for popular movements to get involved in shaping Kyrgyzstan's foreign policy priorities. Central to these hopes was the Issyk Kul movement organised by Chingiz Aitmatov which held its first meetings on the shores of lake Issyk Kul in 1986 and subsequently met in Switzerland, Spain, Mexico and then again in Kyrgyzstan in 1997. At these gatherings leading intellectuals stressed the need to develop a broader understanding of security which would encompass the concerns of ordinary people, with much discussion focusing on environmental protection, public health and the end of nuclear testing.[3] Yet though well meaning organisations of this type may have shaped the rhetoric of President Akaev and other officials, foreign policy retained its traditional dependence upon priorities determined by the political elite.

In developing his foreign policy Akaev was to be supported by the foreign minister, always a personal choice regardless of constitutional niceties. For most of this period the office was held by two individuals, Muratbek Imanaliev and Roza Otunbaeva. The latter held the post for a brief period before being appointed ambassador to Washington, but again took office from May 1994 to the summer of 1997 when she was commissioned to head the Kyrgyz embassy in London. Imanaliev, after a period as ambassador to China, chaired the international department of the presidential administration before once more taking over the foreign ministry which he had briefly led during the first months of independence. The politics of these changes are extremely hard to unravel, and though one commentator rather sardonically commented that Otunbaeva was too nice for the rough world of Kyrgyz politics, her relatively lengthy survival suggests considerable ability, strength and connections.[4]

The day to day handling of foreign policy is left to the foreign ministry—its staff now augmented by a new generation who have been trained in Moscow, Ankara and elsewhere—but the president has retained a firm hand on the broad direction of policy. This dominance has been reinforced in various ways, from the greater role given to the international department of the presidential administration, through the creation of a security council in 1994, to the 1996 constitutional amendments which codified the head of state's responsibility for the shaping of foreign policy. This concentration of policy making in executive hands has come under some criticism from opposition politicians and media outlets but has not generated as much heat as Akaev's gradual extension of presidential power in the domestic sphere. Though individual decisions have been attacked, parliamentary criticism has tended to sidestep the White House (the home of the government and president) and concentrate attention on the foreign ministry itself. In parliament assaults on official policies have tended to concentrate on side issues such as the expense of foreign involvements, as in September 1997 when deputies in the Legislative Assembly suggested that there were too many embassies in European countries and that it might be more sensible to have representation in Siberia or Xinjiang.[5]

The security needs of the new state had been broadly defined in March 1992 by General Janybek Umetaliev, the head of the State Committee for Defence. These included the defending of territorial integrity, protecting the rights of the citizen, preserving the social fabric of the country, the defence of national values and the constitution, and participation in regional cooperation and security agreements.[6] Two years later a presidential decree established a Security Council largely modelled on its Russian counterpart. The decree published in February 1994 emphasised the broad concept of security being used when it spoke of economc and ecological security, the need to combat crime and corruption, and to protect the health of the population. The Council's role was seen primarily as consultative and advisory: to give the president and government advice on how to deal with specific problems and to coordinate the activities of those state organs responsible for dealing with them. Its membership included the president, prime minister, deputy prime minister with responsibility for extraordinary situations and civil defence, the ministers of state security, the interior and defence, and the commander of the national guard.[7] The broad conception of security used by this body was evident at a special meeting held in September 1996 which led to the sacking of some senior officials and severe reprimands for others who had been at best financially incompetent and at worse corrupt. Further meetings in the summer and autumn of 1997 heard reports on the punishment of over 2000 people involved in economic crime, including many law enforcement officers who had been complicit in covering up such activities. At the same time these meetings gave some indication of the broader conception of security being utilised by issuing a document entitled 'the conception of ecological security of the Kyrgyz Republic'.[8]

Nonetheless, however broadly one defines security, all states rely to some extent upon the use or threat of armed force in defending their integrity. This task was complicated in Kyrgyzstan, as in other CIS countries, by the inheritance of single Soviet military establishment whose resources and manpower had to be divided up following independence. Though sometimes amicably achieved, frictions remained. Kyrgyz conscripts continued to serve outside the republic for some time after the attainment of independence, whilst relations with the Russian high command were damaged by events, such as the flight of Russian piloted planes from Kyrgyzstan to Barnaul in Siberia. In addition matters were complicated by the reluctance of many in the predominantly Slavic officer corps to serve in Kyrgyzstan or swear an oath of allegiance to the new state, and the relatively high rates of desertion amongst conscripts. Instability also followed from the uncertainties of the early 1990s which were characterised by considerable fluidity in military organisation as the young state sought to define its security needs and objectives.

Eventually, and after several administrative reorganisations, there emerged four main branches of the Kyrgyz armed forces. The largest of these were the ground forces, formally comprising around 10,000 men, most of them conscripts serving 12–18 months. In addition there was to be a 4,000 strong air defence command (though much of the air fleet was given to Uzbekistan in 1995), an elite National Guard to support the constitutional order, and a Border Guards command made up of around 2,000. With the internal security forces, this gave the republic armed forces that on paper comprised nearly 30,000 men. Nevertheless, problems remained, stemming from a lack of financial support, which meant that the services often did not receive even the severely limited amounts assigned them in the state budget. Simultaneously morale amongst the conscript army remained low, with ill treatment of new soldiers a common complaint and poor food meaning that the vast majority of the Kyrgyz army was in poor health. One consequence of this was that the republic's armed service in the mid-1990s had the highest desertion rate of any of the CIS armies.

Though Kyrgyzstan set about creating its own armed forces, it was accepted that military security could not be guaranteed by the country's own might and that cooperation and agreement with neighbouring states was essential. Kyrgyzstan therefore signed up to the collective security agreements reached at the May 1992 Tashkent CIS summit, and initialed a series of military agreements with Russia, Kazakhstan and Uzbekistan. In consequence the border guards work together with a joint command patrolling the Chinese border—though a recent agreement with Russia means that Kyrgyz border guards would take over responsibility for the main airports and crossing points with China from 1998—whilst Kyrgyz units have been involved in various international actions stemming from the country's membership of the Commonwealth of Independent States. Most notable here have been the activities of a 500 strong battalion under the command of an ethnic Russian on the Tajik-Afghan border—though in the summer of 1997 Vladimir Lukin, chairman of the Russian State Duma's International Committee dismissed Kyrgyz efforts as largely symbolic.[9] Wider cooperation has also been evident in the country's joining with Russia, Kazakhstan, Tajikistan and China in signing agreements on force reductions on their mutual borders during the spring of 1997 and in the decision to participate in the creation of a Central Asian peacekeeping unit under UN auspices which can be made available for action throughout the world and which held its first exercises together with US troops in September 1997. Yet for all this international cooperation, Bishkek has had to remain sensitive to Russian concerns most notably in abandoning any hope of adopting an official policy of neutrality and in formally opposing NATO expansion during General Secretary Javier Solana's visit to the country in March 1997.

ENSURING STABILITY

A primary security concern for any new state, especially a multi-national one emerging from lengthy dominance by a much more powerful entity, remains the maintenance of internal stability. Moreover, many of the problems that face states internally have international dimensions which require that would-be state and nation builders have to take into account the interests and likely responses of neighbouring states in shaping their policies. In the case of Kyrgyzstan a number of issues have come to dominate discussions of security including the question of how to manage actual and potential ethnic conflict, the containment of 'religious extremism', the combatting of criminality and the narcotics trade, and the solution of the refugee problem created by the ongoing conflict in Tajikistan.

As already discussed, concerns about the potential for ethnic conflict stemmed from the demographic inheritance of the new state, with the Kyrgyz making up just over half the population in 1989, though this had risen to around 60% by the beginning of 1997. Two groups of special concern to nationalistically minded politicians were the Russians concentrated in the northern regions and the Uzbeks in the south, seen as potential fifth columns for their mother states and of doubtful loyalty to the new order. The Russian issue has been largely dealt with earlier in the book, and by the middle of the 1990s it appeared that to a greater or lesser extent the Slavic population that remained posed little danger to the republic in terms of promoting overt conflict. Less clear was the position with regard to the substantial Uzbek minority (14.2% of the population in 1996) largely concentrated in the Fergana valley. Some expressed fears that Uzbekistan might utilise Uzbek discontents to interfere in Kyrgyz politics. Needless to say official Tashkent has denied any such intent, with President Islam Karimov repeatedly eschewing any claims on Kyrgyz territory and publicly refusing to back the efforts of those ethnic Uzbeks who agitated for secession in 1992. Nonetheless, tensions remain and Uzbekistan has not been above throwing its weight around at times of crisis, notably following the introduction of the Kyrgyz national currency in May 1993 and during the same year when Uzbek troops on exercise crossed over into the Osh region without seeking prior permission from Bishkek. At the same time Karimov has made it clear that he believes that Uzbekistan has a right to ensure the good treatment of fellow Uzbeks who happen to live across the border.[10] Conversely, there have also been complaints about the treatment of the Kyrgyz minority in Uzbekistan, of whom there are over 150,000, though many of these no longer know their own language. According to some sources Tashkent has embarked upon a process of assimilation, denying this community Kyrgyz language schools and encouraging them to adopt Uzbek as their passport nationality.[11] Yet despite these potential ethnic flashpoints, Kyrgyzstan has so far managed to avoid any repetition of the bloody ethnic violence of 1990.

The other ethnic groups whose presence has major implications for Kyrgyzstan's dealings with the outside world are the Uighurs of whom there are over 40,000 excluding the products of mixed marriages which are not uncommon. These represent but a tiny minority of this Turkic group compared with the seven million plus who live in China, mostly in the neighbouring Xinjiang province, but the activities of some of their organisations have on occasion led to tensions between the two countries.[12] Under Soviet rule organisation was more or less impossible, but under Akaev representatives of the Uighurs have been able to form a number of social organisations devoted to the furtherance of community life. Some of these have focused on Uighur culture, the defence of language rights, and the preservation of traditional ways of life. Others have adopted a more overtly political agenda, criticising

Peking's treatment of the Uighurs within China and in some cases advocating the creation of a separate Uighur state. This in turn has irritated China, coinciding as it does, with the rise of nationalism amongst its own Turkic citizens which has become more acute in recent years and led to outbursts of rioting and violence in early 1997. In such circumstances Bishkek has sought to calm Chinese fears whilst allowing some degree of cultural autonomy to its own Uighurs. In 1992 the Ministry of Justice refused to register one organisation on the grounds that its advocacy of a separate Uighur state represented interference in the internal affairs of China, and in March 1996 the ministry suspended the activities of the Ittipak (Union) organisation on the grounds that it had been encouraging separatism. Yet in January 1997 the less politically active Association of Uighurs was able to hold a congress in Bishkek at which it pushed for greater rights for the community within Kyrgyzstan. On paper this stance appears to satisfy Peking, though the Chinese remain suspicious of activists within Central Asia who help to disseminate information about Chinese policies in this region and give shelter to activists from Xinjiang. This wariness was reinforced during early 1997 when Uighurs were able to demonstrate outside the Chinese embassy in Bishkek following the unrest in Xinjiang. The subsequent strong response to unrest which ensued within this region, involving numerous arrests and some executions, suggested that the Chinese were in no mood to compromise or tolerate any interference in their internal affairs. For their part the governments in Tajikistan, Kazakhstan and Kyrgyzstan promised not to provide any support or refuge for the Uighurs, though the government in Bishkek would still prefer to adopt a more even handed approach in deference to the sensitivities of its largely Turkic population.

The second perceived, some would say imagined, threat to Kyrgyzstan's security comes from 'religious extremism', with events in Tajikistan during 1992 serving to focus the minds of all the region's leaders on the potential mobilising power of Islam. Following the August coup in Moscow, the Communist old guard in Dushanbe had found itself subject to considerable popular demands for change largely articulated by a coalition of nationalist, democratic and Islamic forces. In May 1992 these forces had been brought into a government of national unity which they completely took over for a few months during the autumn. Yet unable to assert their authority country wide, the government was defeated by armed groups supporting the old order and pushed into opposition after a bloody civil war. Forced to set up their base in Afghanistan, the resistance to the new order in Dushanbe becaming increasingly dominated by Islamic groups and it was this fact that was used first by Uzbekistan and then by the Commonwealth of Independent

States to justify intervention to prop up the regime. Simultaneously, it was argued that only firm action against Muslim radicals would prevent the spread of 'extremism' in other Central Asian states and into southern Russia. In Uzbekistan this led President Karimov to crack down on the Islamicist movements that had been developing since the late 1980s, especially in the Fergana valley, and to call for tougher action against radicals on the part of his neighbours. Akaev, however, was less than convinced by this analysis of the Tajik conflict in terms of 'goodies and baddies' and sought from a very early stage to find means of reconciling the opposing sides.

Nonetheless, in Kyrgyzstan, there emerged some public discussion of the possible rise of 'fundamentalist' movements within the republic and their potentially destabilising role. With Gorbachev's liberalisation of religious policy, mosques started to be reopened from late 1989 onwards and by the mid-1990s there were a reported 1,200 active in the republic, most of them located in the Osh and Jalalabad regions. At the same time, the early 1990s witnessed the appearance of religious emmissaries from Pakistan, Saudi Arabia and elsewhere, who put money into the reconstruction of mosques and medressahs and who often propagated a far more radical interpretation of Islam than that practiced by the relatively liberal and syncretistic Kyrgyz. This, as we have seen, led to divisions within the Muslim community, as some leading figures adopted a more puritanical Islamicist vision which the traditionally lax Kyrgyz found unacceptable. More importantly, elements within the security apparatus argued that the rise of movements of this type, however loose and poorly organised, posed a threat to internal stability. Such concerns underlay the replacement of the Kyrgyz mufti at the end of 1996, the expulsion of a number of Islamicists from Pakistan in 1997, and helps to explain the re-certification of imams that took place during the summer of 1997. For all this it is hard to see external religious involvement as seriously threatening Kyrgyzstan's security and certainly none of her immediate neighbours would wish to encourage radical Islam. Talk of an Islamic threat misunderstands the nature of Central Asian Islam, in particular failing to take account of the degree of secularisation of the majority of Kyrgyz intellectuals, the weak penetration of dogmatic religion amongst the people, and the (currently) limited mobilising power of religious slogans in Kyrgyzstan, with the possible exception of the Osh region.

A more substantial threat is posed by the growth of transnational crime, most notably the drug trade. Though Kyrgyz security services have apprehended people smuggling a wide variety of goods, from precious metals to weapons, a far more urgent problem is posed by the passage of illegal drugs. Though the production and useage of cannabis, opium and other drugs has a long history in Central Asia, the exponential growth in the narcotics business dates largely from the Soviet war in Afghanistan during which a number of the regional warlords embarked upon drug related activities in order to fund their military efforts against the Soviet regime. For many the original aim of removing the occupying forces was soon forgotten as they discovered the profitability of their new business, whilst for ordinary people involvement in the cultivation and sale of drugs was often the only means of survival in the midst of war. Simultaneously drugs from Afghanistan began to permeate the Soviet Union, as traffickers crossed the mountainous borders and Soviet conscripts returned to the motherland as addicts or suppliers. The situation was further complicated by the collapse of the USSR and subsequent events in Tajikistan which saw a repetititon of the Afghan pattern whereby warring factions turned to this trade as a means of supporting their military activities.[13]

Within Kyrgyzstan the growth in drug related activities stems in part from the Tajik conflict but domestic factors have also played a role. For many years the republic has been a producer country with thousands of acres of wild cannabis and opium poppies to be found in the Chu valley, the Issyk Kul region and elsewhere. Whilst most of this remained untapped, the growth of social deprivation during the early 1990s has led many to seek a more profitable use for such crops, and for a brief moment at the beginning of the 1990s there was even some public discussion of legalising production. Though this was eventually rejected, the cultivation and sale of narcotics has expanded radically within the republic and provided a major headache for the authorities. Some indication of the scale of the problem can be seen from both the number of registered addicts—which had reached 50,000 in 1995—and the scale of seizures by the law enforcement agencies in the first half of the decade—from 5kg of narcotics in 1991 to 627kg in 1995. The easy availability of drugs was also indicated by falling prices, especially in the south, with a kilo of opium in Bishkek reportedly costing twice as much as in Osh. This in turn pointed to a regional dimension as nearly half of illicit drugs were found in the southern Osh region, and the town itself appearing to have become the major trading point for this lucrative trade. According to some official sources this was not surprising given the role of regional bosses in the area, and there were allegations that the powerful southern politician Bekmamat Osmanov was a key player in the drug trade. There were also repeated claims that the militia in Osh was led by people who made a living from the business, or who turned a blind eye to the activities of those who ran it. Such claims were apparantly confirmed by a series of arrests in 1997, which saw senior members of the Osh militia accused of participation in such activities. Nonetheless, such claims were bitterly rejected by Osmanov and other southerners who saw it as part of a northern plot to discredit their region.[14]

Whatever the truth of this matter, it is clear that despite recently heralded successes against the Osh branch of the industry, dealing with this problem is extremely difficult. The collapse of the USSR and civil war across the border has made it far more difficult to control or police territorial boundaries. The main Khorog-Osh highway which links Tajikistan with Kyrgyzstan quickly became a major supply route for drugs and one which presented particular policing problems. During much of the year sub-zero temperatures render the available sniffer dogs ineffective, whilst the road is policed by poorly paid militia men subject to both temptation and coercion. As one law enforcement officer put it, to effectively control the drug trade on this road it would take officers every few hundred yards, each of whom was guarded by another. When traffickers succeed in passing this road their prime destination is generally the southern town of Osh which appears to have become a major distribution point for the whole of Central Asia. As in other parts of the world the drug barons are able to use those facing poverty and deprivation who are tempted to risk their freedom for potentially large profits, whilst others have been coerced into becoming carriers by regional bosses or criminal gangs. In such cases the law enforcement agencies are able to apprehend the mules but find it hard to touch the main culprits. The latter have been aided, in at least one recent case, by the support of a senior official in the security services. Even when such people have been arrested it has often proved virtually impossible to convict them, especially if trials are held in their own regions. Thus, in the summer of 1997, it was not surprising to find the Kyrgyz Procuracy trying, albeit unsuccessfully, to move the trial of the Osh militia officers involved in the drug trade outside the region because the key witnesses were being threatened or bribed to keep silent.[15] In such circumstances it seems likely that the Kyrgyz state is going to face an uphill and long term struggle to deal with this major threat to its internal stability, which also raises serious questions about its ability to police its own borders.

The conflict situation in Tajikistan has created other difficulties, with fears in the early 1990s that fighting might spill over the border and that an influx of refugees could also create serious problems. Though the republic participated in various CIS peacekeeping efforts, Akaev from the beginning of the conflict called on both sides to make concessions in pursuit of peace. Within Kyrgyzstan public opinion was divided, with many uneasy about being drawn into somebody else's war, especially as this appeared to involve propping up a government with territorial claims on parts of southern Kyrgyzstan. In

April 1995 an article in *Slovo kyrgyzstana* asked how Kyrgyz interests were involved and suggested that it might be time to reduce the size of the Kyrgyz battalion protecting Tajikistan's southern borders. Though recognising the need to protect the ethnic Kyrgyz fleeing from the Pamirs, it warned of the potential for a major refugee crisis if the conflict was not brought to an end and feared the impact of violence spreading northwards.[16] These fears were exacerbated by occasional reports of armed bands active in the south of the republic, and the appearance of larger number of refugees than the government could cope with.

By early 1997 the United Nations High Commission on Refugees was reporting 17,000 registered refugees—mostly Kyrgyz from northern Tajikistan of whom there are 50–60,000—but to this should be added over 25,000 unregistered Tajiks, located mostly in the south. In 1995 the UN agency opened offices in Bishkek and Osh and cooperated with CIS migration agencies and the Kyrgyz government in developing programmes to reduce the possibility of ethnic conflict, provide work and housing, and funding various seminars and summer schools on tolerance and human rights. Yet articles in the Kyrgyz press during the spring of 1997 suggested a considerable groundswell of resentment directed against ethnic Tajiks who were seen as promoting violence and criminality in the republic and taking away jobs and homes from ethnic Kyrgyz.[17] Despite this the Kyrgyz government appeared willing to maintain a relatively liberal refugee policy and in October 1996 became only the 5th of the Soviet successor states to accede to the 1951 UN Refugee Convention and its 1967 Protocol. This elicited considerable praise from the UN commissioner Sadako Ogata when she visited the region in May 1997, though at the same time she added to Kyrgyz fears when warning that the advances of the Taliban in Afghanistan might create a new wave of refugees fleeing into Central Asia.

Continuing tensions in Tajikistan meant that many refugees, especially the ethnic Kyrgyz, were likely to remain within the republic despite the limited economic opportunities available to them. Nonetheless, by June 1997 hopes were being expressed that any further flood could be avoided in consequences of the various peace deals which Akaev had played a role in mediating during the previous months. Under these agreements it was hoped that political reconciliation would allow the return of most refugees to Tajikistan, though much will depend upon the ability of both sides to restrain armed groups and the durability of any peace deal. Moreover, continued conflicts in Afghanistan with their knock on effects in Central Asia mean that refugees are likely to remain a major issue for all the Central Asian republics well into the next century.

NEW FRIENDS, OLD ALLIANCES

Whilst taking steps at home to combat any threats to internal stability and security, the young state also spent much of the early 1990s seeking to develop links with the wider world. To this end it has sought to balance traditional ties to the former Soviet world with the search for new partners capable of contibuting towards Kyrgyzstan's political and economic reconstruction. Writing in the government newspaper *Nasha gazeta* in May 1997, academician Turar Koichuev suggested that Kyrgyzstan had five options in resolving the problem of national security. The first involved declaring positive neutrality under the flag of the UN, though how practicable this was in the face of Russian objections remained unclear; the second would be to enter a defence union with the former Soviet states of Central Asia, on paper a much more likely option given their common heritage and traditions; the third which entailed union with Turkey and other Turkic states he saw as unrealistic give the lack of territorial connections and real common interests; the fourth involving a defence pact with China he saw as equally impractical as the two peoples have very different mentalities and traditions; and the fifth, rooted in a long historical association, lay in signing a defence pact with Russia. Given the historical experience and existing ties of a military and economic nature it was the second and fifth of these that he saw as forming the linchpin of Kyrgyz security until well into the next century, and as effectively already underlying relations within the CIS.[18]

Though this analysis accurately described Kyrgyz orientations during the early 1990s it omitted any real discussion of the search for partners and security guarantors within the industrialised world. From the very beginning official Bishkek expressed hopes that the West, in the broadest understanding of the term, might be able to offer some degree of support for any restructuring programme. It was this hope that led the republic to seek membership of a wide range of international organisations, and to adopt a market rhetoric that it hoped would lead to investment within the country. The same imperative led Kyrgyzstan to join such unlikely organisations as the Conference on Security and Cooperation in Europe and even for a while speak of the future prospects of joining NATO. The latter was never really on the cards and, though Kyrgyzstan did join the Partnership for Peace programme, in early 1997 it offered formal if unenthusiastic support for Russia's efforts to prevent the expansion of NATO. Of special concern to Kyrgyzstan has been the development of relations with the United States, a feeling that has evidently been reciprocated to some extent by a Washington which until the mid-1990s bestowed special favour on this 'island of democracy'. Up until then tiny Kyrgyzstan received larger per capita subventions through agencies such as USAID than other Central Asian states, but by 1996 the US was expressing concern at perceived restrictions on political freedom as well as shifting to a 'realist' position which recognised that whatever its human rights record Uzbekistan was a far more important regional player than Kyrgyzstan.[19]

A further orientation pointed to by Koichuev was one that focused on relations with Turkey. The collapse of the Soviet Union following on from the postponement of Ankara's hopes of entry into the European Union led to considerable euphoria following the rediscovery of Central Asian 'brothers and sisters' in the early 1990s. Much was made of common historical and linguistic roots which might lead to a new union of Turkic nations. Whilst the initial enthusiasm soon dimmed in the face of vast cultural differences, Kyrgyzstan has joined other Central Asian states in seeking close ties with Turkey. Regular summits have been held at which the Turkic states have issued broad proclamations of the need for unity, cooperation and collaboration in the resolution of political, economic and environmental problems. Equally attractive has been the largely non-religious nature of Turkey's 20th century development project and following an August 1995 meeting in Bishkek the Turkic heads of state issued a communique including a firm commitment to secularism. Yet though Bishkek has sent army officers and diplomats to train in Istanbul and Ankara, and despite some Turkish involvement in the construction and telecommunications field, the relationship has not been as productive as many might have hoped. Equally, the commitment to secularism has not prevented Kyrgyzstan from developing good relations with more radically Islamic states such as Iran. Particularly important were growing trade relations with the republic's southern regions, which led to Teheran opening a consulate in Osh in mid-1997. Nonetheless, as we have seen elsewhere, there remains a certain wariness of Muslim countries that have been sending 'missionaries' to the region, with the security services keeping a close eye on the activities of islamicists from Pakistan and other parts of the Muslim world.

Relations with Beijing have been more complex, as China has become a prominent actor in the region but publicly eschewed any intention of replacing Russia as the major influence. The dealings between the two countries go back centuries and have not always been easy, with the Kyrgyz on occasions subject to Chinese overlords who have persisted with claims on parts of Kyrgyz territory. Relations are also complicated by ethnic politics with around 140,000 Kyrgyz in China's Xinjiang province, mostly the descendants of those who fled after the 1916 revolt. To this should be added the previously discussed Uighur problem which has complicated relations between Bishkek and Beijing. Despite these complications, formal relations have remained civil as the collapse of the USSR led to increased economic and political con-tacts between the two countries. By the mid-1990s China was the country's largest trading partner after Russia and was more willing than most states to exchange goods on a barter basis. China was able to supply considerable quantities of foodstuffs, clothing, electrical products and basic consumer necessities such as matches; in turn she received the products of metal work-ing and hydro-electric power, with the two countries signing major agree-ments on the construction of water processing facilities. In addition China has played a key role in the construction of a new highway running from Osh which will facilitate trade relations between the two countries. At the same time the two countries have been able to resolve many of their border con-flicts, largely in the context of CIS-Chinese negotiations.

Evidence of sensitivity to Chinese concerns has been evident in various ways, not least of which has been the considerable warmth with which visit-ing Chinese dignitaries are greeted—evident at the time of the visit of the Chinese defence minister in June 1997 when Lenin avenue was renamed after Deng Xiaoping. Aware of Kyrgyzstan's vulnerability to pressure from its mighty neighbour, Kyrgyz leaders regularly express their understanding of Chinese positions on international issues such as the status of Hong Kong and Taiwan.[20] Yet many Kyrgyz remain wary of China, suspicious that sub-stantial sections of the economy are coming to be dominated by Chinese businessmen and noting that in the Naryn region and Bishkek these same people have been very active in buying up real estate. Despite the desire to escape Moscow's tutelage there is a feeling that falling under Beijing's influ-ence would be far less desirable.

For all these new ties, relations with the Soviet successor states have re-mained paramount since the achievement of independence. During the early 1990s Bishkek remained wary of schemes for regional cooperation, fearing that she might be in danger of seeing her interests subordinated to those of her larger and rather more ambitious neighbours. Though at the Bishkek summit of Central Asian leaders in April 1992 there was some talk of closer ties, most of the region's leaders seemed unconvinced or, in the case of Turk-menistan with its huge natural gas potential, positively hostile. Nonetheless, during 1993 and following the crisis over Russian monetary policies which led to the introduction of national currencies, Kazakhstan, Uzbekistan and Kyrgzystan began to move closer together. In 1994 the three presidents signed an agreement to create an economic union, partially based upon the EU example, which proclaimed their committment to creating a common market with shared policies in certain defined areas. Various institutional structures were created and summits of leaders, prime ministers, foreign ministers to be held on a regular basis. In many cases these amounted to little more than statements of intent, but by 1997 there was on paper a Central Asian Bank, some measure of agreement on how to respond to the crisis in Afghanistan following the advances of the Taliban movement, and an agreement to create an inter-parliamentary council. Some journalists in Bishkek were suspicious about the proposals to create a common information space which they suspected would be based on the tightly controlled Uzbek model. In addition there were questions about how the economic union might be affected by broader integration efforts within the USSR, with Kazakhstan and Kyrgyzstan joining a customs union with Russia and Belarus which Uzbekistan's leader viewed with undisguised hostility.

Despite formal and informal moves towards integration, there remain tensions between these states, stemming from traditional rivalries, differing political styles and temperaments, and the sometimes contradictory demands of economic reform and nation building. Particularly problematic are Kyrgyzstan's relations with Uzbekistan, not helped by the very obvious 'elder brother' complex of many leading officials in Tashkent. Though some Kyrgyz politicians point to the relative economic success of Uzbekistan, others are suspicious of President Islam Karimov's authoritarian style while he in turn has little time for the quasi-pluralistic politics of his neighbour. Yet there are also substantive issues at stake which render some degree of conflict inevitable. Though Karimov has denied any intent to interfere in Kyrgyz political life, or question existing borders, events have occasionally given the lie to such idealistic proclamations. For example, in December 1992 Tashkent's security services appeared to act with impunity in seizing Uzbek dissidents on Kyrgyz territory, and during 1993 Uzbekistan held military exercises in the Osh region without Akaev's prior approval. Tensions were also evident at the time the som was introduced in May 1993, and on various occasions since then Uzbekistan has cut off gas supplies to Kyrgyzstan when it failed to pay for resources already provided. Difficulties may also follow the June 1997 decision of the Kyrgyz parliament to charge Uzbekistan and Kazakhstan for water from Kyrgyz reservoirs. Though the government in Bishkek has stressed that this is something which needs to be negotiated rather than unilaterally determined, Tashkent had at the time of writing largely ignored Kyrgyz requests for serious discussion of this issue. Relations with Kazakhstan seem less problematic, although official negotiations over the issue of water supplies had also reached a stalemate by September 1997.

More fundamental, however, may be the conflict between pressures for integration and the demands of nation building. In a recent article Paul Kubicek noted the importance for the Central Asian states of carving 'out their own space' and the 'need to imbue their states with a distinct national flavour, differentiating themselves from their neighbours and, hopefully, giving birth to a sense of common identity'. In such circumstances the pursuit of closer cooperation may indeed by counter-productive, threatening the attempt of Kyrgyzstan and others to build a new nation state in a very fragile world.[21]

Whilst pushing for a greater degree of regional cooperation, Akaev has from the very beginning stressed the centrality of relations with Russia which stem from the historical ties of the two peope and the fact that Moscow remains the republic's chief economic partner. In part influenced by many years working in Russia, Akaev has been concerned to push home to his countrymen the reality of their situation. There may be considerable sympathy for Kyrgyzstan in the outside world, especially in the United States, but nobody was going to guarantee Kyrgyzstan's security or economic well being. For this reason she remained dependent in many areas on good relations with Russia. This became even more important from mid-1993 as Moscow started to adopt a more assertive policy in the 'near abroad'.[22] In the political sphere this entailed taking up the issue of ethnic Russians in the successor states, with claims of ill-treatment and discrimination being frequently levelled by Moscow. With regard to Kyrgyzstan this meant in the first instance pressurising the republic into rethinking its attitude to the status of the Russian language. During the 1993 discussion of a new constitution it was made public that Moscow's ambassador to Bishkek had delivered a letter from Yeltsin to Akaev stressing his concern over the language issue. Though this did not lead to any amendment of the constitutional position, Moscow's sensitivities as well as a realisation of the importance of retaining Russian speakers may have prompted Akaev to push hard for a recognition of the official status of Russian from 1994 onwards. Equally, official Bishkek has been far more tolerant of Russian political organisations than some of its neighbours, registering at least some cossack organisations and the Movement for Brotherhood and Union which is quite explicitly committed to the restoration of some form of single union. Though some within the Kyrgyz elite have proved sceptical of moves to placate Russia, notably on the language issue, all have recognised the need to go through the motions of flattering Russian sensibilities. Equally Russia has continued to make it clear that the needs of the Russian speaking population must be respected and has not been above somewhat unsubtle diplomacy, as in the decision of the speaker of the Russian parliament to visit Bishkek in June 1997 at the very moment when the Kyrgyz parliament was due to vote on whether to amend the constitution so as to make Russian an official language.

Economically the dependency relationship built up over seventy years continues to have an impact upon the relationship. Kyrgyzstan remains not only dependent upon the former metropol for many of its basic goods, but also finds itself in considerable debt to Russia. It was for this reason that Bishkek signed up to a customs union with Russia, Belarus and Kazakhstan in March 1996, and at around the same time granted Russia substantial holdings in a number of tobacco companies and light engineering firms in exchange for cancellation or reduction of debts.

In the military sphere Moscow has rejected Akaev's earlier inclination to neutrality and insisted that she be involved in the security arrangements of the republic, something that also suits official Bishkek. Treating the southern borders of Central Asia as effectively its own, Moscow has maintained its own border guards along the Chinese border—though this will change to some extent in 1998. It has also bargained hard on behalf of ethnic Russian officers who in the early 1990s occupied many of the leading positions in the Kyrgyz armed services. Under agreements reached in 1994 Russian officers serving in the Kyrgyz army will be entitled to leave the republic at the end of their tour of duty and to be re-housed at the expense of Kyrgyzstan in any part of Russian except Moscow and St Petersburg. From Kyrgyzstan's perspective many of these measures represent necessary concessions. Yet at the same time they remind the political elite and population alike that the relationship between the two states is extremely uneven: Kyrgyzstan may need Russia, but Russia has no absolute need of Kyrgyzstan.

1 Quoted in S. Harden, ed., *Small is Dangerous: Micro States in a Macro World* (London, Frances Pinter, 1985), p. 4.
2 There are now a considerable number of studies of the international politics of Central Asia, including: A. Banuazizi & M. Weiner, ed., *The New Geopolitics of Central Asia and its Borderlands* (Bloomington and Indeanapolis, Indiana University Press, 1994); P. Ferdinand, ed., *The New Central Asia and its Neighbours* (London, Royal Institute of International Affairs, 1994); M. Mandelbaum, ed., *Central Asia and the World* (New York, Council of Foreign Relations, 1994); M. Olcott, *Central Asia's New States: Independence, Foreign Policy and Regional Security.* (Washington DC, United States Institute of Peace, 1997). J. Anderson, *The International Politics of Central Asia* (Manchester, Manchester Univerity Press, 1997) provides a more general introduction to Central Asian politics rather than international relations in the strictest sense.
3 See the discussion of this theme in T. Tashybekov, *Narodnaia diplomatiia i stanovlenie vneshnei politiki suverennogo Kyrgyzstana,* (summary of candidate's thesis for the Russian Academy of Management, Moscow, 1993).
4 The change is reported in *Nasha gazeta* 4 July 1997; officially Otunbaeva left at her own request.
5 Reported in *Turkistan Newsletter* 30 September 1997.
6 Quoted in R. Wolff, 'The armed forces of Kyrgyzstan', in *Jane's Intelligence Review*, May 1994, p. 230.
7 This decree can be found in *Slovo kyrgyzstana* 4 February1994.
8 Cf. *Nasha gazeta* 1 & 5 August 1997, and 23 September 1997.
9 In an interview with the radio station 'Ekho Moskvy' on 11 August 1997, a translation of which was circulated on the CENASIA mailing list, 14 August 1997.

10 *Nezavisimaia gazeta* 15 May 1992.

11 Z. Sydykova, *Za kulisami demokratii po-kyrgyzski* (Bishkek, 1997), p. 84.

12 For a general survey see Justin Rudelson, 'The Uighurs in the future of Central Asia', in *Nationalities Papers*, 22:4, 1994, pp. 291–309.

13 For a general discussion of the drugs trade in the former USSR see *Transition*, 20 September 1996.

14 *Slovo Kyrgyzstana* 8 April 1995.

15 Cf. *Central Asian Post* 22 May 1997; *Delo No* 4 September 1997.

16 *Slovo Kyrgyzstana* 15 April 1995.

17 See *Vechernii Bishkek* 12 May 1997.

18 *Nasha gazeta* 7 May 1997.

19 S. Frederick Starr, 'Making Eurasia stable', in *Foreign Affairs*, January–February 1996, pp. 80–92.

20 Radio Free Europe/Radio Liberty, *Daily Report*, 19 June 1997.

21 P. Kubicek, 'Regionalism, nationalism and *realpolitik* in Central Asia', in *Europe-Asia Studies*, 49:4, 1997, pp. 637–55.

22 On this gradual policy shift see N. Melvin, *Forging the New Russian Nation* (London, 1994), pp. 27–48.

Bibliography

Compared with the coverage of many other Soviet republics, there is a very limited amount written about Kyrgyzstan in English. This very select bibliography points to a few general works on Central Asia and cites some key articles on the history and politics of Kyrgyzstan. Its does not include the many Russian language sources used in preparing this text.

Achylova, R. 'Political culture and foreign policy in Kyrgyzstan', in V. Tismaneau, ed., *Political Culture and Civil Society in Russia and the New States of Eurasia* (New York, 1995), pp. 318–36.

Akiner, S. ed. *Political and Economic Trends in Central Asia* (London, 1994).

Akiner, S. *Islamic Peoples of the Soviet Union* (London, 1986).

Allworth, E. ed. *Central Asia: 130 Years of Russian Dominance* (3rd edition, Durham, N.C & London, 1994).

Anderson, J. *The International Politics of Central Asia* (Manchester, 1997).

Anderson, J. 'Constitutional development in Central Asia', in *Central Asian Survey*,16: 3, 1997, pp. 301–20.

Anderson, J. 'Elections and political development in Central Asia', in *The Journal of Communist Studies and Transition Politics*, 13: 4, 1997, pp. 28–53.

Banuazizi, A. & Weiner, M., ed. *The New Geopolitics of Central Asia and its Borderlands* (Bloomington & Indianapolis, 1994).

Dabrowski, M., et.al 'Economic reform in Kyrgyzstan', *Communist Economics and Economic Transformation* 7: 3, 1995, pp. 269–97.

Ferdinand, P. ed. *Central Asia and its Neighbours* (London, 1994).

Gleason, G. *The New Central Asian States* (Boulder, 1997).

Howell, J. 'Coping with transition: insights from Kyrgyzstan', in *Third World Quarterly*, 17: 1, 1996, pp. 53–68.

Huskey, E. 'The rise of contested politics in Central Asia: elections in Kyrgyzstan, 1989–90', in *Europe-Asia Studies* 47: 5, 1995, pp. 813–33.

Huskey, E. 'The politics of language in Kyrgyzstan', in *Nationalities Papers*, 23: 3, 1995, pp. 549–72.

Huskey, E. 'Kyrgyzstan: the politics of demographic and economic frustration', in I. Bremmer & R. Taras, eds, *New States, New Politics: Building the Post-Soviet Nations* (Cambridge, CUP, 1996), pp. 654–80.

Imart, G. 'The Islamic impact on traditional Kirgiz ethnicity', in *Nationalities Papers*, 14:1–2, 1986, pp. 65–88.

Mandelbaum, M. ed. *Central Asia and the World* (New York, 1994).

Olcott, M. *Central Asia's New States: Independence, Foreign Policy and Regional Security* (Washington, 1996).

Pannier, B. 'Islam's tenuous hold in Kyrgyzstan', *Transition*, 29 December 1995, pp. 26–8.

Pannier, B. 'President acquires more power in Kyrgyzstan', in *Transition*, 2 January 1996, pp. 94–5.

Pannier, B. 'A linguistic dilemma in Kyrgyzstan', in *Transition*, 29. November 1996, pp. 28–30.

Pomfret, R. *The Economies of Central Asia* (Princeton, 1995).

Pryde, I. 'Kyrgyzstan: the trials of independence', in *Journal of Democracy*, 5:1, 1994, pp. 109–20.

Pryde, I. 'Kyrgyzstan's slow progress to reform', in *The World Today*, June 1995, pp. 115–18.

Wolf, J. 'The armed forces of Kyrgyzstan', in *Jane's Intelligence Review*, May 1994, pp. 228–31.

Index

Abdrakhmanov, Yu, 12–13
administrative division of
    Kyrgyzstan, 4–5, 9
Afghanistan, 91, 93
Agrarian Labour Party, 34, 38
agriculture, 2, 5, 11–12, 65–66,
    73–75, 80–83
Aitmatov, Ch., 12, 17, 52, 86
Aitmatov, T, 13
Akaev, A., 20–21, 23–30, 33, 36,
    38–42, 45, 47–50, 52–56,
    59–60, 65, 68–70, 72, 75–6,
    83, 86–87, 92, 94, 100–101
Akmataliev, T., 61
Alexander the Great, 1
Alianchikov, A., 58
Amanbaev, J., 27, 34, 53, 57, 69
Andreev, I.I., 4
Andropov, Yu, 17
Arabaev, Ch, 62
army, 88–89, 101
Asaba, 35–36, 38
Ashar (Mutual Help), 19, 32
Asian Development Bank, 74,
    76, 78
Assembly of the Peoples of
    Kyrgyzstan, 49
Ata Meken, 35, 37–38, 52
Aybalaev, M., 53

banking, 72–73
Bishkek, 32, 37–8, 80, 83, 93–94
Bolsheviks, 8
Brezhnev, L., 15
'Bukhara' organisation, 8

Canada, 77
Chagatai, 1

China, 1, 3, 7, 43, 77, 89–91,
    97–98
Cholponbaev, M., 53
Christianity, 33, 44, 56
Chu region, 23, 27, 38, 40, 93
Chyngyshev, T., 27, 36
civil society, 29–39, 62
clans, see tribalism
Clinton, H., 58
Commonwealth of Independent
    States, 70–71, 83, 89, 92
Communist Party, 13–15,
    17–18, 31, 34, 37–38,
    52, 69–70
constitution, 25–27, 48–50
corruption, 72, 75, 80–81, 87–88
cossacks, 31, 36, 46
currency reform, 70

Democratic Movement of
    Kyrgyzstan, 19–20, 34–35, 38
Democratic Party of Women, 36
drugs, 66, 83, 92–94

economic development, 5–6,
    10–12, 16, 65–84
economic integration, 78–79,
    98–99
elections, 21, 24–25, 50–54
emigration, 44–47
Erkin Kyrgyzstan, 35–38
European Bank for Reconstruction
    and Development, 74, 76

Fergana valley, 2, 5, 8–9, 12,
    33, 66, 90, 92
Free Economic Zones, 76, 84
Frunze, M., 8–9

Germans, 44, 46
gold production, 27, 76–77
Gorbachev, M., 17–21, 92
Great Patriotic War (1941–45),
    14, 66

homelessness, 19, 32
Howell, J., 83

Imanaliev, M., 86
industry, 11, 16, 66–68
International Monetary Fund,
    69, 73, 76, 78
Iran, 97
Islam, 3, 10, 12–13, 16, 25–26,
    33, 56–57, 63, 91–92
Issyk Kul movement, 86
Issyk Kul region, 5, 38, 59, 67,
    76–77, 80, 93
Ittipak, 91

Jalalabad region, 8, 19, 38, 40,
    43, 61, 70, 81–82, 92
Japan, 78
Jews, 46
Jumugalov, A., 18, 27

Kaptagaev, E., 56, 63
Karabekov, K., 62–63
Karimov, I., 43, 70, 90, 99
Kazakhstan, 71, 78, 83, 89, 99
Kenjakunov, M., 59
Khrushchev, N., 14
Koichuev, T., 41, 96–97
Kokand, 3–4
Kriminal, 40, 58
Kubicek, P., 99–100
Kulov, F., 25, 27, 72
Kumtor gold field, 27,
    76–77
Kurmanjan-datka, 4
Kyrgyz in Uzbekistan, 90
Kyzyl-Kiia, 7

land reform, 54–55, 75
language issue, 15–16, 19–20,
    26, 43, 47–49, 54–55, 100
Ligachev, Ye, 18
Loitsev, V., 6
Lukin, V., 89

Manas, 3, 61
Masaliev, A., 17–18, 20, 29,
    34, 40, 52–54
mass media, 29–30, 55–56, 58, 60
Ministry of Justice, 31, 35, 58, 90
Mongols, 1–3
Movement for Brotherhood
    and Union, 34, 100
Movement for Deliverance
    from Poverty, 57
Muraliev, A., 36

Naryn region, 8, 32–33, 37,
    40, 54, 76, 82, 98
Nasha gazeta, 96
National Unity of Kyrgyzstan, 21
NATO, 89, 96
Nazarbekov, I., 56

Ogata, S., 95
Omurzakov, Y., 58
Osh aimagy, 20
Osh region, 7–8, 12–13, 16,
    19–20, 38, 40, 42–4, 54, 70,
    72, 81–2, 90, 92–94, 98–99
Osmanov, B., 40, 93
Otonbaeva, R., 86–87

Pakistan, 92
Panfilov division, 14
parliament, 23–28,
    50–55, 58, 87
Party of Unity of Kyrgyzstan,
    36, 39
political parties, 34–39
Pomfret, R., 68

poverty, 81–82
privatisation, 69, 71–71
Procuracy, 59

Qarakhanids, 1

Ramphal, S., 85
referenda, 28–29, 54
refugees, 94
religion, general, 32–33,
    56–57, 91–92
Republican Peoples Party,
    36, 38, 40
Res publika, 30, 55, 59
revolution (1917), 7–9
Russia, 4–6, 67–68, 71, 80,
    89, 100–101
Russians, 14, 45–49, 88, 90

Sarygulov, D., 41, 58
Saltyganov, T., 6
Saudi Arabia, 92
Security Council, 58, 87–88
Semenov, P., 4
Semirechie region, 4
Shalieva, T., 36
Sherimulov, M., 28, 53, 57
Slavic Fund, 47
Slovo kyrgyzstana, 29, 53, 95
Social Democratic Party of
    Kyrgyzstan, 36–8, 52
social organisations, 30–32
Soglasie, 47
Soros Foundation, 58
Stalin, 8, 11–14
Stamkulov, T., 57–58
State Defence Committee, 87
Steppe revolt (1916), 7
Sultanov, M., 73

Svinikhov, I., 6
Svobodny gory, 30
Sydykov, A., 13
Sydykova, Z., 58

Tajikistan, 33, 89, 91–95
Tajiks, 42–43
Talas region, 8, 37–8, 40
Tekebaev, O., 35, 52–53
tribalism, 2, 10, 39–42
trade unions, 31, 70
Turgunaliev, T., 25, 35,
    41, 53–54, 57–58
Turkey, 77, 86, 97
Tursunbai, B., 35, 39
Tynstanov, K., 13

Uighurs, 31, 42–43, 90–91
Umetaliev, J., 87
unemployment, 18–19, 67, 81–82
United Nations High Commission
    On Refugees, 95
United States, 96
USAID, 78
Unkovsky, I., 4
Usubaliev, T., 15–18, 40, 52
Usupov, J., 57
Uzbekistan, 70–71, 78–79,
    83, 89–90, 97–99
Uzbeks, 9, 15, 19–20, 42–4, 90
Uzgen, 1, 20

Valikhanov, Ch, 4

welfare provision, 81–82
World Bank, 71, 74, 76–78, 81, 84
women, 12, 32, 55, 81–82

Yntymak (Agreement), 32, 59, 83

For Product Safety Concerns and Information please contact our EU
representative GPSR@taylorandfrancis.com
Taylor & Francis Verlag GmbH, Kaufingerstraße 24, 80331 München, Germany